Second-Chance
CATS

Books by Callie Smith Grant

Second-Chance
CATS

True Stories *of the* Cats We Rescue
and the Cats Who Rescue Us

Callie Smith Grant, ed.

Revell

a division of Baker Publishing Group
Grand Rapids, Michigan

© 2020 by Baker Publishing Group

Published by Revell
a division of Baker Publishing Group
PO Box 6287, Grand Rapids, MI 49516-6287
www.revellbooks.com

Printed in the United States of America

Library of Congress Cataloging-in-Publication Data
Names: Grant, Callie Smith, editor.
Title: Second chance cats : true stories of the cats we rescue and the cats who rescue us / Callie Smith Grant, ed.
Description: Grand Rapids, Michigan : Revell, [2020]
Identifiers: LCCN 2020001224 | ISBN 9780800735722 (paperback)
Subjects: LCSH: Cat owners—Religious life. | Cats—Religious aspects—Christianity—Anecdotes.
Classification: LCC BV4596.A54 S43 2020 | DDC 242—dc23
LC record available at https://lccn.loc.gov/2020001224

21 22 23 24 25 26   7 6 5 4 3

To the rescuers and the rescued
and to cat lovers all over the world

Contents

Introduction

Callie Smith Grant

I have had many cats in my lifetime, and they were seldom chosen. Many showed up at my door somehow, or an unfortunate situation presented itself, and a strange cat became my cat. They got a second chance at life, and I got a new friend.

The first cat I remember was a feral black tom, though my grandmother called him wild. He would sit outside the kitchen window, leaning against the glass for warmth, and that wild boy would watch me, the small child, eye to eye. I could never pet him, but even through the window, I felt he was my friend. Over the years, various stray cats showed up at my family's country home— silvery grays, tabbies, and gingers. They moved in and became my buddies. My mother rescued a pretty tuxedo girl from a situation we would call animal hoarding today, and that cat slept on my bed every night during my teenage years. When I was in college, my roommate saw someone throw a pillowcase from a moving car—a pillowcase full of three terrified kittens, all of whom we kept and loved. And there were many more.

For twenty years, I have been writing about these animals, and for much of that time I have also collected other writers' true stories for book compilations about cats, dogs, or horses. A few years ago, I approached my publisher with an idea of compiling true stories about animals of many species who rescue humans in some way. Was the publisher interested?

Kind of.

The publishing committee liked the rescue theme, but they preferred the book be only about dogs. I considered that, then suggested two compilations instead—one about rescue dogs and one about rescue cats. The committee responded that they still wanted only the dog book because "people don't think of cats as rescuers."

Hmmm. I understood why they said that, and I realized I had work to do. The second part of being a rescue cat is getting the chance to pay good things forward to their humans and even rescue them in various ways. I'd seen that happen.

We went ahead with the dog book, which became *Second-Chance Dogs*. Later I brought up the cat idea again, this time with a broader meaning of the word *rescue*. I included a couple of true narratives that showed how some humans rescue cats and how these cats rescued them back in their unique feline ways. The committee saw this as something exciting to sell, and that book became *Second-Chance Cats*. Simply defined, these are the cats who show up—for a new home or a new relationship. Then they show up again—to provide companionship, respite, stability, and more.

In this collection of true stories, some cats are rescued from shelters. Some are plucked from homeless litters. Cats are rescued from parking lots and even from a big box store. One little guy is literally snatched up from the middle of a road. Sometimes a child brings home a cat, sometimes a spouse brings one home, sometimes another animal brings home the cat. Or sometimes the cats, being proactive kinds of beasts, decide for themselves who's going to "rescue" them by arriving at the right place, right time. Or the right place, wrong time, and that's another story . . .

We meet cats from humane societies and shelters, kittens being sold out of a box, cats presenting themselves at the worst time or at the best time. Sometimes they travel long distances to arrive at a doorstep by mysterious, sometimes jaw-dropping, means. They help with the care of humans and sometimes other animals.

We also meet cats with physical disabilities who make wonderful pets. Cats with blindness, deafness. Cats with diseases kept at bay who live full and happy lives. Amazing feral cats who develop community relationships with each other. Cats who turn people from cat-neutral to cat-positive. Cats who clearly improve the daily lives of those who know them.

So do cats rescue? You bet they do, and you'll read about them here. It can be subtle when they let humans know something is amiss and needs tending. They pay forward the consideration given them by rescuing children and adults from loneliness. They help the young, the aged, the physically impaired, the mentally ill. A few times, in this book, the rescue is more direct. A cat finds an abandoned litter of kittens that humans are searching for. A cat helps a couple of humans stay alive. Literally. And some of these cats help each other too.

So the committee got the book they believed they could sell. Storytellers got to honor their cats by telling their stories. And I had the privilege of pulling together a heartwarming collection. If you know and love cats, I am happy to report that you are about to meet some very cool cats—some who may seem familiar to you and some so amazing you couldn't imagine them existing. That happened to me, and I've been a cat lover since I was a toddler.

I know these are stories you'll love to read and pass along. Enjoy!

1

Lady Finds a Lap

Lonnie Hull DuPont

When I was in high school, a friendly, long-legged ginger tomcat appeared at the back door and decided to stay. He had some scars and was not young. But what a nice guy he was. When it was clear he was moving in, we got him neutered and vaccinated. He became an indoor/outdoor cat at our house and lived a happy rest-of-his-life with us.

He won Dad over right away. I'm convinced cats zero in on who needs to like them. Fortunately, Dad was hooked. He named the cat Tom and turned him into sort of a dog-cat who followed him all around our property. Tom would leave his window naps anytime he heard Dad pull a coat from the back door closet and run to join him. He hung out in the garage while Dad tinkered on cars. He slept on Dad's lap during TV time.

Tom came to Dad immediately when called by name, the first cat I knew to do that. At night, I would stand at the back door and call Tom home the way my grandmother taught me—"Here kitty-kitty-kitty-kitty-kitty . . ."—fast like an auctioneer until I was out of breath. Then I'd suck in more air and start over. At which time, Dad would have me step aside, and he'd call, "Tom." If necessary, he'd add, "Tom Cat." That's all it took, and here came that leggy boy, loping in from the back fields, chatting at Dad the whole way.

I would stay at the back door and keep calling for our other cat, Boots, who would show up in her own good time. She was that kind of cat, a strong-willed, serious hunter turned living room diva. She had not been thrilled about Tom moving in, but she adjusted. They were not great buddies, but they got along well enough, as a neutered male and a spayed queen often do.

If our cats didn't appear when called at night, there was a way for them to get into the house without all the in-and-out drama. Dad left a broken basement window covered in vines unfixed, making an unusual but effective pet entrance. Since our farmhouse was well over a hundred years old and few inside doors would close all the way anymore, our cats could paw open doors to get to and from the basement.

Eventually Boots passed away, and then we had only Tom and my parents' small dog. I never knew Tom to pay much attention to Boots while she was alive, but it appeared he was feeling a loss of some kind for his own species. I say that because, within days, he literally brought home another cat.

On that day, Tom appeared from the basement via the laundry room and wound up in the kitchen, where he loudly meowed. We discovered he'd brought a friend with him—a black-and-white short-haired female I'd never seen before. She bore a cut on her face, a weepy eye, and a messed-up ear. She right away urinated on the rug, and Tom yowled at her until she seemed sufficiently shamed. Dad approved of her, so we whisked her off to the vet to get her injuries treated. She came home to be christened with the name Lady by Dad. And a lady she was indeed. She turned into a big, beautiful tuxedo cat with round topaz eyes rimmed in her natural black eyeliner.

Now that Tom had replaced Boots and rescued his new injured friend, he apparently considered his work done. He ignored Lady from then on.

Dad and I were fond of Lady and both talked to her. She was very warm toward us, purring and looking into our eyes. But Mom never took to her. All but one of our pets over the years were strays. Mom only had one pet she chose herself, and that often annoyed her. She was good to our pets, and she had always liked Tom. But for some reason, not Lady. Mom claimed that she was tired of cleaning up after shedding cats, so she made a new rule that Lady was never to leave the kitchen, except to go through the basement to the outdoors.

Lady was given a chair of her own in the kitchen. Since this room was an active hub, at least she was around people. But she sometimes seemed more of a fixture than a pet. She dealt with it graciously, though every now and then she ventured forth into the living room, only to have my mother say, "Oh no you don't." Then Lady would twirl around and head back to her kitchen chair as if she had intended to do that all along.

After college, I moved back home for a couple of years. During my first winter back home, we lost Tom to old age. A few months later, my folks took their dog and headed south for a winter of warmer weather. Now it was only Lady and me, holding down the fort together in the old house.

During our winter together, I had no desire to confine Lady to the kitchen, so I let her explore and tiptoe about. She seemed only interested in the dining and living rooms. She curled up on the couch with me while I read, and she was a big love with a deep purr. I had two wisdom teeth pulled that winter, and that turned into an unexpectedly painful situation for a weekend. I probably should not have been alone for that, especially with the negative way I reacted to codeine. But Lady was with me—attentive, purring, and curling up on my lap or sleeping with me on the couch. She was a wonderful distraction and truly a caring presence.

After spending the winter with Lady, I decided that this sweet tuxie girl needed a home where she could be what she truly was—a sociable lap cat who wanted to get off that kitchen chair and be someone's beloved companion. While I never understood my Mom's behavior toward this nice cat, I did know it wasn't going to change. So I took it upon myself to look for a new home for Lady.

The first re-homing didn't work out, and to this day I feel awful about it. I didn't know the people that well—friends of friends—which was my mistake. Lady would not venture forth in her new home, which is fairly normal behavior for a cat in a new place. She immediately hid, and that particular household had no patience for it. They called me the next day to take her back. I had chosen the wrong home for this lovely girl.

So I picked Lady up, and I'll never forget how subdued she was on the drive back home. I could feel her uncertainty. I apologized to her and said I'd do better next time.

Next time was the right time. I mentioned wanting to find Lady a home to an old high school friend, and he said his elderly grandmother lived alone and might be interested. She was indeed. We took Lady to her new home several miles away from my folks' house, and although I hated to say good-bye, I knew this was going to be the home where Lady could shine. She knew it too; this time she didn't hide.

So Lady landed on her pretty feet once again, as some cats manage to do. When after a few months I asked about her, my friend said his grandmother had just bought Lady a new rhinestone collar.

We were all happy for her. Even Mom.

2

The Cat in the Living Room

Maggie Marton

There's a cat in my living room."

I heard the tension in my husband John's voice on the phone, but I couldn't wrap my mind around what he was saying.

"What?"

"A cat! There's a small black cat standing in my living room."

I paused. "Okay," I said. "How?"

He told me that moments before, he had heard meowing outside his door. He opened up to peek, and there stood a tiny black kitten. She took one look at him and waltzed in.

He assumed she was a few months old. Her petite, slender body and enormous triangular ears belied her age. He would later find out that she was about a year old, but her tiny stature—and the mischievous personality he'd soon discover—made her seem kitten-like.

Summers in Louisiana sizzle. The scorched ground and oppressive humidity turn people into water bugs, skittering from one air-conditioned location to the next. This kitten, John knew, needed help to survive the mid-July heat. So, after he hung up the phone, he drove to the nearest pet store and stocked up on cat stuff: a litterbox and litter, cans of food, toys, and a water dish.

In this Louisiana town, stray cats lurked around every corner. John knew the ferals who lived in and around his apartment complex. This cat, though, he'd never seen before, and she was just so small. He assumed someone was looking for her. He hung up signs, posted online, and joined a lost pets Facebook group. She was sweet, he said, and looked fairly healthy, so she had to have people, right?

Yet, as much as he wanted to help her, he didn't want to keep her. When John was a child, he developed a fear of his aunt's cats who swiped and bit at his legs. That ultimately became a general fear of cats. I'd always wanted a cat. When I was a child, my mom said no. So now that a cat came to my husband, I thought this was my chance.

But at the time, I lived nine hundred miles away in Indiana.

Earlier that year, at the tail end of winter, John received his first and only job offer after completing his PhD in environmental science: He was to work in the bayou, studying the effects of the Deep Water Horizon oil spill. At the same time, I received news that, yes, that spot on my back was cancer. I needed to start a year of chemo at the end of February, a few weeks before John's start date. We struggled to reconcile these two facts, and in the end, the need for health

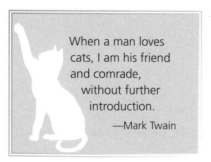

When a man loves cats, I am his friend and comrade, without further introduction.

—Mark Twain

insurance through John's job won out. He'd move to Louisiana while I stayed in Indy to receive my treatment. He planned to commute back and forth for a year, then once my treatment ended the following February, I'd move down with our three dogs.

That spring, John loaded his Saturn Ion with an inflatable mattress, a stool, clothes, a set of dishes and cutlery, a lamp, and reference books. He planned to buy a futon when he arrived in Louisiana two days later. He leased an apartment sight unseen over the phone. He filled out his HR paperwork while I sat in the cancer center getting my daily two-hour chemo infusion. Then, he left.

Sure, it was the logical plan, but it proved to be difficult for John. The sicker I got, the harder it became for him. He felt helpless, he said over our nightly Skype call, and frustrated that he couldn't do anything. Plus, he felt isolated and lonely in a new home.

Months passed. He loved his job, but he struggled with the rest.

And then the kitten appeared.

Because of John's fear, it shocked and delighted me that he welcomed this small cat into his place. He called her Newt, a nod to his favorite sci-fi movie. He spent the next few months terrified of his new roommate. He slept with his bedroom door closed, afraid to pet her, unsure of how to spend time with her. Meanwhile, he searched for her family.

Weeks passed. No one called.

"Toss her in the bayou," folks told him. "Alligator food," they said.

Meanwhile, he found a veterinarian. Newt had worms and fleas. She was underweight. She wasn't spayed. On the day of her spay, she cried in her crate so mournfully and broke his heart so completely that he called me that afternoon and said, "Okay. So we have a cat."

When he picked her up after her spay, she hadn't fully recovered from the anesthesia. She crawled into his arms, and he cradled her like a baby until she awoke fully.

Since John traveled back to Indiana as often as possible, he interviewed pet sitters to take care of Newt. During their first meeting, one pet sitter played with Newt and scratched her belly.

"Aren't you afraid she'll bite you?" John asked the pro.

"No," he said with a laugh. "Newtkins is the sweetest!" He tickled her belly again and tossed a piece of crumpled paper that Newt chased and pounced on and kicked. John hired that sitter on the spot.

Newt quickly became John's "princess." He spoiled her with treats and toys, and he talked about her nonstop. When he flew back to Indiana, as soon as his plane landed, he'd whip out his phone and scroll through dozens of pictures of Newt doing cat things. "Here she is asleep on the futon, and here she is playing with her pouncer, and here she is just sitting there."

When he was back in Louisiana, he'd regale me with Newt stories each night on Skype. He'd pan the camera around the living room so I could watch her pounce on her toys or, more often, sit perfectly still and stare at John. Sometimes he'd set up his laptop so that I could watch him play with her and her teaser toy. "Look how high she can jump."

He texted me daily with pictures of Newt playing with feathers and jumping in and out of a packing box. He emailed me funny stories from Newt's day: "She figured out how to open the kitchen cabinets, so now she hides and pops out to startle me. I think she does it to be funny."

Newt started a daily game of "hide the dish sponge." When John left for work in the morning, the sponge sat on the drying rack in the sink. Late afternoon, he'd return home and the sponge would be gone. He'd poke around to find it and replace it in the sink, only for Newt to repeat the game the next day. It made John happy; he'd text me the locations of the pilfered sponge most weekdays.

She chewed through the cord to the ceiling fan, which lost him his security deposit. She popped his air mattress, so he spent the rest of his time in the apartment sleeping on the floor. Newt, meanwhile, slept on the cushy futon. I teased John about being too afraid to cuddle with her to sleep on the futon mattress. He was afraid she might bite him, he said, like if he rolled over on her in the night. But he was comfortable enough to swap his jeans for a pair of shorts because he was pretty sure she wasn't going to attack his legs now.

He developed nicknames for her: Newtie, Newtie-tootie, Newtie-tootie-fresh-and-fruity, Newtles (sounds like "noodles"), Toots, Toots McGoots, and Newtkins, the name bestowed by the pet sitter. Most often, though, he called her "my pretty, pretty princess."

And every day upon his return home from the lab, he'd open the door to Newt sitting on the other side awaiting his return.

One crisp fall morning, I sat in my oncologist's waiting room with my mom. The week prior, I underwent another CT scan to see if the cancer had spread to my lungs or abdomen. While I waited to be called back, my phone dinged. It dinged again. And again. I pulled it out of my purse and opened my messaging app.

John had texted a string of photos—Newt with her tongue stuck out from three different angles. I laughed. I turned the phone to my mom to show her the silly photos. My mom smiled.

"That cat," she said, "is John's guardian angel."

I finally met Newt the following summer. I finished chemo at the end of February, and it took three months to pack up our Indy house, find a rental in Louisiana that accepted three big dogs and a cat, and hire movers to get us those nine hundred miles.

25

John found and moved into the new place a few weeks ahead of time to help Newt adjust to her new home and to set up the basics. Then John flew up to drive from Indy to Houma with me and the dogs.

We drove the eighteen hours over two days, and when we arrived at the rental, John took the dogs in the yard while I went inside to meet Newtie, one on one. I perched on the edge of the futon. She eyed me while I held still, letting her set the pace.

She crept over and sniffed my hand. I didn't move or speak until I felt like she grew bored of me. As she started to walk away, having gotten a thorough whiff of me, I whispered to her, "Thank you, Newt. Thank you for keeping John safe."

And then I silently apologized for the three dogs she was about to meet . . .

3

The Gift

Andi Lehman

Stray cats and kittens covered the sloped brown yard like fallen leaves from a tree. As I picked my way up the cat-covered hill, I wondered how I would ever choose just one. I scanned the furry faces for the special friend I needed. My parents waited on the road below me, both hoping my choice would solve a major problem for us all.

Ever since the US Navy transferred our family to Ankara, Turkey, I had dragged home every homeless cat I could find. Big or little, friendly or not-so-friendly, each cat I saw became "my cat." Tabbies, gingers, calicos, black, white, or brindle—it didn't matter. They all seemed to call my name.

My folks had tried to reason with me. Feral cats could scratch and bite. They carried diseases that could hurt me, my brother, or my newborn sister. It was dangerous for a seven-year-old girl to wander around alone in an urban neighborhood filled with political unrest and poverty.

But I couldn't help myself. I loved cats. Stuffed animal kittens and cat figurines littered my bedroom. Pictures of cats cut from magazines and posters of tigers and lions adorned the walls. I memorized the entire text of my favorite book, *The Contented Little Pussycat*. I was a cat-crazy kid, and I wanted a real one.

I spied cats everywhere, sitting on the fence in our backyard or poking through the garbage cans next to our apartment building. They lay on the steps going up to our third-floor flat. They frequented the meat market just down the street where they fought over the raw renderings thrown aside by the vendors.

My father grew tired of putting homeless cats back where I found them, and my mother wearied of explaining that Ankara didn't have animal shelters like we did back in the states. My concerned parents decided a cat of my own might thwart the steady stream of strays.

So here I was, choosing my first pet from a lawn full of felines kept by a local woman who fed them. Their swishing tails made the ground look alive with fuzzy fingers. A few cats watched me with narrowed eyes as I approached, but most turned away from my gaze and moved if I drew close to them.

Midway up the hill, I spied a multicolored, long-haired kitten tucked behind a rock. I thought he was the most beautiful thing I'd ever seen. When I bent to touch him, he opened his eyes and blinked sleepily at me. He didn't scratch or squirm as I picked him up. Purring in my arms, he sealed his future. I had found my forever friend.

My father grunted when I brought my pick to the car to meet him. "That's the grungiest-looking cat I've ever seen," he said. Despite my initial protests, the name stuck, but Grungy came home with us. He delighted my parents by curbing my wanderlust in search of a buddy, and I didn't really care what name we gave him. I adored Grungy.

Unfortunately, my new charge liked to roam at night. He got into more mischief than a roomful of unsupervised toddlers. He fought with other cats and came home more than once bleeding and battered. Like his feral counterparts, he frequented the garbage cans despite the wholesome meals we fed him. That bad habit cost him a broken leg and several days in a Turkish animal hospital after the garbage truck ran him over one misty morning.

But I never brought home another stray after Grungy moved in with us. He slept on my bed, came when we called him, and ruled over the other critters we acquired for my siblings. Grungy inserted himself deep into the din of our family's life symphony. He moved with us to our next duty stations in both Rhode Island and Florida.

We had lived in Key West for two years when doctors discovered the cause of my chronic bronchitis: allergies to nearly everything, including my best friend. My parents made the difficult decision to rehome our pets, even Grungy. I cried when the new owners came to pick up my cat. I couldn't imagine a life without animals. How would I survive without the cat who had filled the kitten-shaped hole in my heart?

The young couple who adopted Grungy lived two islands away on Boca Chica Key. They might as well have lived in China. I knew I would never see Grungy again. My sadness deepened when we learned he had run away from his new home. An exhaustive search failed to find him. No one knew if Grungy was alive or dead, and I struggled not to imagine the worst.

I dreamed often about the cat who had slept at the foot of my bed and sat on my desk while I did homework. I overheard my parents talking in hushed whispers about me. Just as they had worried about my physical health in Turkey, they worried about my emotional health now. We hoped things would improve when I started seventh grade in the fall.

Months later, on a bright October morning, I headed outside for the short walk to Horace O'Bryant Junior High. As I stepped down into our carport, I nearly tripped over a thin, pitiful figure meowing on the doormat. I set my books on the workbench and turned around, eager to pet the stray cat after a whole summer without one. As my hands reached down to touch the grizzled head, I heard the unmistakable thrumming sound of contentment, and familiar green eyes looked up at me. I scooped Grungy into my arms, buried my face in his matted fur, and sobbed.

We children went late to school that day. We brushed and fed Grungy while my mother called his owners to tell them the amazing news. Everyone marveled at my cat's determination to come home. How had he traveled miles of elevated ocean highway and crossed three Florida Key towns? More importantly, what would become of him now?

I begged my parents to let us keep him. He wanted to be with our family—that was clear. If he couldn't live in the house with us because of my allergies, could he be an outdoor pet? I thought I would die if I had to say good-bye to him again.

I spent every free moment with Grungy while I waited for the verdict. When it finally came, I cried with joy over his triumph. The young couple who lost Grungy agreed to give him back to us. If he could be content to live on our patio or in the carport, he could stay. And stay he did. Grungy moved with us twice more, first to Texas and then to Virginia before he passed away at thirteen.

Since the fateful autumn day when Grungy completed his miraculous journey back to our family, I have always lived with at least one pet. Today, I enjoy the company of more than twenty. By coming home with us in Ankara and by finding his way back to us in Key West, Grungy granted me a precious gift. He gave me a life with animals—not just once, but twice.

Forever.

4

Parker the Dad

Robbi Hess

There is the cutest cat down here at the groomer's."

These were the words that sealed our fate with the kitten we'd eventually name Parker. My husband should have known any phrase that starts with "There is the cutest cat . . ." would lead to my running down to the groomer's and checking out said kitten.

The kitten was at the groomer's because of a special relationship the groomer had with the local animal shelter. They'd bring kittens and cats to the groomer because her grooming business and pet store had lots of foot traffic. Many cats and kittens found new homes there.

The ginger and white kitten was there with his two siblings, but it was the kitten's golden-eyed beauty that caught our eye. I'd never seen a cat with gold eyes before. Although he wasn't the most outgoing of the bunch, the kitten captured our attention because of his unique look.

My husband and I spent some time with the kitten at the groomer's, playing with him and cuddling him. Within an hour, we'd filled out the paperwork, paid the adoption fee, and brought the kitten home. We kept telling ourselves we didn't need another cat. Apparently we did need another cat because we just happened to be there when Parker was available. His other siblings had been spoken for, and maybe Parker was still there because he wasn't outgoing or very playful. But we took a chance on this kitten who'd been left behind.

At the time Parker joined our family, we had two older cats—Jessie and Claudia—and a large husky-shepherd mix named Spenser. Even though Parker was the youngest and the smallest of our pets, he quickly took on a unique role in our household. He became "Dad" to all the other pets.

Parker would bathe the older cats. Sometimes he tried to physically pin them down to do this. The two older kitties were very placid—they indulged Parker by lying down and letting him wash their faces and ears. Eventually the washing turned to roughhousing and would end up with Parker puffing his little body up and hopping sideways, hissing and spitting. Claudia and Jessie were unperturbed by his antics.

Our dog Spenser, who weighed in at more than one hundred pounds, would defer to Parker when he came hopping toward him. Spenser allowed Parker to chew his ears and play with his tail.

As Parker grew older, we added more kittens to the family. I have a soft heart for lost or forgotten or homeless kittens and rarely say no to giving one a home. I've taken in kittens who were supposed to be short-term fosters who became forever family members. I have never considered them "foster fails" but instead "foster wins." The fosters won by joining our home, and we won because they stole our hearts and filled us with joy.

At one point when we had five cats, our daughter brought home a kitten she'd found at a farmer's market and hid him in her bedroom. She thought we wouldn't notice the kitten paws reaching out from under the door when she went to school. The cat family in the house then bloomed to six.

While our older cats Jessie and Claudia didn't embrace the newcomers to the household with any kind of gusto, Parker did. It never mattered the age or sex of the newcomer, Parker took on the role of "Dad" and washed each and every pet in the house every day.

When I rescued my mini-poodle, Henrietta, from a puppy mill, Parker even took care of her. At the time Henrietta came home, Parker outweighed her by more than ten pounds. But he was gentle with her when he could have easily considered her prey.

Spenser tolerated the cat houseful. One day he inadvertently stepped on one of the kittens who was jumping around his legs. The kitten, Mickey, howled, and Parker came racing toward Spenser and the kitten (who was not injured). Parker, the eleven-pound cat, backed our hundred-pound dog into a corner, hissing and slapping at him. Spenser lay down on the ground, belly up, and Parker backed off. Fewer than ten minutes later, Parker had comforted the kitten, then lay down next to Spenser. Order had been restored.

Seven years ago I went through breast cancer surgeries and treatments. Parker joined my poodle in the chair with me while I rested, cried, and tried to heal. He would gently stand on the arm of the chair, purr, and bump his head against me. He kept the other cats off me and seemed to be protecting my battered body from their antics.

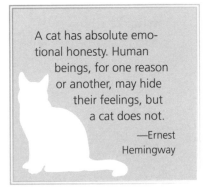

A cat has absolute emotional honesty. Human beings, for one reason or another, may hide their feelings, but a cat does not.

—Ernest Hemingway

When Spenser became ill four years ago, Parker seemed to be the first to know. My husband and I were puzzled by the way Parker would wrap himself around Spenser's head when he lay down. Parker would follow Spenser around the house all day and sleep next to him at night.

On Spenser's last day with us, he was unable to stand. Again, Parker went to Spenser, wrapped his entire body around the dog, then lay his head on top of Spenser's. When we came home from the vet that day without Spenser, Parker dashed around the house howling. Then he came to us and lay on our laps, purring. I am convinced he was doing his best to comfort us in our time of need.

Parker is now sixteen years old and is slowing down. But he continues to take care of us all. He remains our furry alarm clock and never fails to come into the bedroom, walk on our pillows, and bump against our heads five minutes before our alarms go off. He jumps onto the bathroom vanity and watches while we get ready for work, then races us to the back room for breakfast with the other younger kitties in the house, Ickis and Oblina. Parker still washes the other cats, and we often find Ickis and Oblina snuggling next to him.

This rescue cat has filled our hearts and our home for so many years with his big "Dad" personality. He chirps to us when we talk with him, and he struts around the house like he is the one in charge of it all.

And he still is.

5

My Cat for a Day

Claudia Wolfe St. Clair

On this beautiful Sunday morning I wake early. My summer routine usually begins with a walk through my vegetable garden to check on its growth. New sprouts and blooms on the tomatoes and squash all point to future harvest and enjoyment. Another wave of mayflies has settled on the house and the underside of leaves in the garden. The breeze comes from the northeast off Lake Erie; diamonds sparkle on the water's surface.

Sitting in the shade at the picnic table, I think back to another summer when life here was less than idyllic.

After my parents' passing, the family home was used as a rental property. A massive rainstorm caused damage inside and out. The basement had flooded. Leaks became an issue around the windows that faced the lake. Cracks in the stucco deepened, and weirdest of all, paint was blown off the surface of the house. It became a summer spent tackling each necessary repair.

Once the flood cleanup was dealt with, the logical next step was to stabilize the structure of the house. The cosmetic issues would come later. With an estimate in hand for stucco repair, the course of the summer was signed on the dotted line. Movable scaffolding went up and work began.

Scraping paint revealed more cracks. Lots more. The original paint saw the light of day. The house had been painted pink, which was typical of an art deco house of the 1930s. Over the years the art deco aspects of the structure had been removed and replaced. In its current condition it looked like a derelict Texaco gas station with its pumps missing. Being on the waterfront was its only saving grace.

As further scraping continued, exposing even more cracks, the costs went up every time the scaffolding was moved to a new section of the wall. My labor on the project did little to rein in the rising expenses. It was physically exhausting and mentally draining.

On a windless day, with the sun directly overhead, I climbed down from the scaffold for a break. Actually, I came down to cry. Dreading the mounting costs, I was in tears and in pain. Every muscle hurt.

I dragged a chair to the edge of the break wall where I sat down and let the tears fall. Would this ever end?

How would I pay for all of this?

Out of the corner of my eye I noticed something moving. It was a cat, walking straight toward me with resolve. In all the weeks of work, I had never seen this cat before. The shade beneath my chair seemed to be his objective.

He was a good-sized, ginger-colored tabby cat. He had a large square head and amber eyes. Folded ears lay close to his head. There was a bend in the cat's tail from a long-healed injury. He seemed content to rest in the shade.

I wiped away a few tears and sat marveling that I suddenly had feline companionship. Meanwhile my ginger buddy began stretching and rolling around as if engaged in some ritual. What a life! Not a worry in the world. I envied the cat.

As if he could hear my thoughts, the cat emerged from under the chair and sat down at my feet. We sat in companionable silence just looking at each other.

Cats and I had never mixed before, so this experience was completely new to me. The cat was at ease with me, and so was I with him.

Suddenly he jumped into my lap. Well, that was unexpected! With his front paws he marched up my chest to look into my eyes up close. He licked the tear salt from my cheeks. He nestled under my chin, inviting more contact. As I scratched behind the cat's ears, he settled into my lap to allow further attention. He dozed off.

We sat like that a long time. I have no idea how long. The anxiety and worry seemed to draw away while the orange tabby purred and slept. My muscles relaxed. I was calm and felt at peace. It was a perfect moment.

Something I have learned over time is to notice when a perfect moment presents itself. There are gifts in such moments. It's as if the hand of God rests fleetingly on your shoulder for reassurance. Hand of God? A cat on my lap? A gift.

After some time, the ginger tabby roused. He looked up at me and jumped down. He looked once more before he turned toward the overgrown weeds at the edge of the yard. He sauntered back from whence he had come. I watched him go. He did not look back. I never saw the cat again.

Over the course of that summer I fell in love with the house again. Repairs were slow but steady. There were solutions to the rising costs. At some point I decided I would move back into the family home.

This morning at the picnic table I think about the cat. The place where he had emerged from is now a shade garden, the weeds and debris all banished.

Other animals are regulars in the yard. A groundhog lives at the edge. I've seen a fox wander through and a weasel. Lots of rabbits call the place home. Neighborhood feral cats manage the rats and mice. Squirrels continue to extort peanuts. Cranes and seagulls swoop low across the break wall and an occasional bald eagle as well. Birdsong fills the air. But the tabby never returned.

It makes me wonder about the nature of angels, especially as I sit here today—happy, at peace, and making new memories in this house by the lake, where the heights of children and grandchildren are marked on the wall.

I've come to believe that sometimes an angel comes on four feet, with bent ears and a broken tail. He looked at me with amber eyes and took in my tears. He wasn't meant to stay forever. I believe he was an angel sent to be my cat for a day.

6

Meeting Miss Daisy

Leanne Lowe

The clouds were gray and heavy as we drove to the new town. I thought we would never arrive. I was pretty confident we were moving to the middle of nowhere. Everyone else in my family seemed to be full of enthusiasm over this new town named Jonesville. The name alone reminded me of stories we learned in history about cults. My adolescent mood was as sullen as the sky.

The despair mounted as we drove down the dusty brown dirt road and stopped at the gaudy two-story mint-green box that was to be our new home. There was no civilization in sight, only hewn-down cornfields in every direction. I was lamenting the loss of my lifelong best friends. I missed dressing up and dancing to Madonna's "Material Girl," hanging out at Dave's Place with the best pizza and burritos anywhere, the park, the pool, the Dairy Queen, my life on wheels with both roller blades and my bike, and pretty much anything that resembled civilization. I felt like I was in teenage purgatory.

I'd love to write that once we met our neighbors, life improved. However, for a country block, which is to say a four-mile radius, every neighbor kid was a boy. I saw all thirteen-year-old boys as awkward and smelly, and I thought country boys were especially dirty as a result of catching snakes, fishing, and running around firing BB guns at one another. Instead of Dave's Place, there was the Magical Farmers 4H Club. All good farm boys owned binoculars, and they paid my younger brother a dollar to let them spy into my bedroom until my dad found out. This resulted in my barricading myself in the house—and a lifelong habit of insisting my drapes always be closed. The consensus was: I *hated* Jonesville!

One day I had had enough, and I refused to attend the neighborhood Magical Farmers meeting. My folks decided to let me stay home alone. Once they left, I headed downstairs and opened the front door, allowing the sunlight to shine in.

I was heading to the kitchen when I heard a cat. I turned around and walked back to find an orange barn cat on the stoop. She had recently given birth to a kitten, and she carried it with her. The umbilical cord was wrapped around its fragile little neck. The momma cat kept looking at me with insistent eyes as if to ask for help. I was terrified.

But one result of living in farm country was that we had studied mammal birthing in school. I hurried into the house and found a pair of scissors and some rubbing alcohol. Back outside, I sat down beside the momma and baby and gently picked the sticky wet mass up and tried not to squirm from the grossness. I carefully clipped and unwrapped the cord. I then handed the kitten back to Momma, where she began to preen her baby and motivate circulation.

Before long, the baby was a mewling fluffy little striped kitten. I named it Tigger right away. Then I named Momma Miss Daisy after my childhood cat. I went back inside and got a small bowl of milk and some tuna for Miss Daisy. She sat there, nourishing herself and watching over her kitten for about fifteen minutes. Then she did the most peculiar thing—she left the kitten with me and meandered off. I again was panicking because there was no way my dad was going to let me keep a cat.

Suddenly, the momma was back, carrying another baby, which she dropped off with me. She kept taking trcks into the weeds behind the garage, bringing babies up that I held in my lap despite the fact that they were making me a little itchy. All in all, she brought me six babies. Once she had gathered all her babies, she stretched out in the sunlight on the porch and rested until her babies demanded her attention. After many long months, I had made my first friend in our neighborhood.

Now the struggle would be to figure out how to hide a litter of cats without my parents or the hoodlum boys discovering them. As Miss Daisy and I basked in the sunlight, the solution was plainly visible. Right in front of me was the old windmill house. I walked over and found a rock to prop the door open, took some straw from my dad's hunting dog's supply, and made a nesting area for the little family. This seemed to meet Miss Daisy's approval. The babies were safe.

One of my daily chores was to feed my dad's hunting dog, so no one ever questioned me taking scraps of meat outside. Each day I'd bring snacks to Miss Daisy, who thanked me by letting me cuddle her babies. I had named each of them despite being unaware of their gender. Tigger's siblings were named Sassy, Tabby, Jasper, Buttercup, and Garfield. Our conspiracy was safe for a few weeks until one of the boys wondered if the windmill might have salamanders and discovered the little family. Before the boys could terrorize anyone, I promptly took command of the cats and locked them on the back porch.

My brat kid brother went running to my dad to tell him what I had done. Knowing I needed to think quickly, I did what all daddy's girls know how to do best. I turned on the tears and sad eyes and followed it up with, "But Dad, I love them!" This is the one weapon all girls can use to get a loving father to cave. For a few more weeks he let me keep them, during which I was able to find new homes for all.

I may have rescued the kitten, but Miss Daisy saved a lonely teenage girl who needed a friend.

7

The Wrong Kittens

Susan C. Willett

Name?"

Pen in hand, I tried to focus on the form in front of me as tears clouded my vision.

"She doesn't have one yet." I looked through the bars of the travel crate at the tiny ball of black-and-white fur buried deep within a blanket. "I've had her less than a day."

"We need a name." The woman behind the counter pointed to the empty spot on the paper. "For our records. You can't leave that blank."

Claire, I wrote. And then in parentheses: *Not Final.*

"Please have a seat in the waiting room. The vet is with someone else and will see you as soon as she can."

It was the Saturday of Labor Day weekend, and we were the only souls in the emergency veterinary clinic waiting room. I sat down on a plastic chair of institutional green and lifted my un-named kitten out of the crate. She felt like a bird, all thin ribs and no weight, as I settled her and the blanket into a nest in my lap. I could feel her tiny purrs.

It was only a few weeks ago that I was at our regular vet's office with Jasper, my hound/lab/whatever mix, who had a recurring problem that required yet another round of surgery. While we were waiting to be seen, we stopped to look at a half dozen kittens sprawled around a cat cage.

Kittens are a great distraction when you don't want to think about your dog's surgery—or the fact that your youngest child was leaving for college in less than two weeks. As we stared into the cage, canine and human minds elsewhere, a splotchy black-and-white kitten jumped up onto a shelf and rolled over onto his back. He stuck his paw through the bars of the cage, little jelly bean pads turned upward, as if asking me to rub his belly.

I reached through the bars with my finger and complied, and then scratched the black patch under his chin. The kitten purred, looked me straight in the eyes, and defied me to explain why I couldn't bring him home.

"I already have three dogs and two kitties." Jasper nosed me in agreement. "That's enough, really." The kitten held my gaze. My elder daughter Corinne's voice echoed in my ears as I remembered her threat to call an intervention if I adopted any more pets. "I'm sorry, Kitten. I just can't."

Over the next two weeks, as Jasper recovered and my youngest daughter Melanie packed for school, I kept thinking about that kitten. I called the vet, and they told me that he and his sister had been waiting quite a while to be adopted—longer than usual. I dragged my husband to meet them and seriously began consider-ing adopting both. Because by then I had realized that adopting two was actually better for all involved. The kittens could amuse

46

each other when I wasn't home . . . and hopefully wouldn't annoy the older cats quite as much.

I hadn't planned on any more pets, telling everyone I was full. But somehow I had gone from No More Pets to Just Two More.

My adoption application was accepted.

On the Friday afternoon of the long Labor Day weekend, I left work early to pick up my new family members. One of the techs brought out the little girl cat first. She was smaller than I remembered, but I thought it was because I had two big cats at home. Then another tech brought out the boy cat.

Something didn't look right. "Wait a minute. Wasn't there black fur on his chin?"

"Oh no! You were looking for the other kittens? One of the vets adopted them; she felt bad that they were waiting so long for homes. This is a different pair. They're still brother and sister."

These were the wrong kittens. They were not the ones I had come for, the boy cat who had chosen me, the only reason I was adopting them to begin with.

"I am so sorry." The tech held the male kitten under her chin protectively. He stared at me dolefully.

At home, a safe room had been set up to welcome two kittens. I had bought new beds and scratchers and toys for them. My husband and I had no plans for the long weekend so I could acclimate the babies to their new environment.

"Do you want to spend some time with these guys instead? No pressure, really. You don't have to adopt them. But since you're here already . . ."

I spent the next half hour on the floor of an empty exam room with two completely different kittens. The boy cat had a black mask and nearly all-black back with a white belly and paws. The tiny female had a triangular shape of white over her left eye, and large splotches of black throughout her body that made her look like a Holstein cow. I watched them explore, chase each other, knock into a trash basket, sneak up and pounce on cat toys.

My husband wasn't answering his phone. An empty weekend loomed in front of me. I had to make this decision on my own.

The door opened and I stood up as the tech walked in. "We're getting ready to close for the weekend. Did you decide what you wanted to do?"

I looked down as the masked one—the male—rubbed figure eights around my ankles. I took a deep breath and simply opened myself to possibilities.

Maybe . . . maybe this was how it was *supposed* to play out. Maybe the wrong kittens were really the right kittens. Maybe the original kitten was no more than a player in whatever story needed to unfold.

I took them home.

On the drive, I began to think about what to name them. I had picked out names for the original pair of kitties: the male was going to be Max, as he reminded me of the troublemaker in the children's picture book *Where the Wild Things Are*. And the female seemed like a Chessie, named after the cat logo for the shipping company Chessie Systems. Those names belonged to the other felines as far as I was concerned, and I had to start all over. I needed the right names for the wrong kittens.

That night, I settled my new babies into a gated kitten-outfitted bathroom—their safe place to learn the smells and sights and sounds of our multispecies home, and for my current menagerie to get to know them. Sitting on the floor, I let the two kittens explore the small space and climb all over me.

I called Corinne that night, imagining her hanging out with her boyfriend Luke in her shoebox-sized dorm room as I sat in the bathroom with the kittens. After convincing her not to hold an intervention—it wasn't that difficult, as we're all animal lovers—we discussed potential names. I told her I was thinking of calling the female something birdlike, since she felt so light and delicate when I held her. I ran through a list of black-and-white birds. Maybe Magpie? Or Adélie, like the penguin. But the cat didn't look chubby like a penguin and that name just didn't fit. That's when Luke said, "You should name her Claire."

Ah yes, the character Claire from the TV show *Lost*. In one of the early episodes of the series, when strange animals like polar bears began appearing out of nowhere on the island, I was convinced that there was a penguin in the rustling bushes of the jungle; I can't remember why I was so sure. Anyway, I was wrong; out of the bushes came a character named Claire. My family thought it was hilarious—and it became a standing joke in our house whenever we didn't know something: "Maybe it's a penguin, Mom."

The logic from Luke was that the kitten was not a penguin, so she should be Claire.

I told them I'd think about it. I wasn't sure I wanted my kitten's name to memorialize a moment in which I was the butt of a joke.

But the next morning I had other issues to deal with; I woke up to find nasty messes all over the bathroom floor, and it didn't take long to realize that the little girl kitty was sick.

Not eating. Diarrhea. Hunched over. Lethargic.

I was relatively new to living with cats; my first two had been with us for just two years, and I never had kittens this young. But I knew that it's dangerous for cats—especially young kittens—to not eat. It was a holiday weekend, my vet's office was closed, and I couldn't reach the adoption group.

This is how I found myself in the emergency clinic with my tiny nameless kitten.

For more than an hour and a half I sat with not-really Claire on my lap. She barely moved. Her eyes were squinted shut. My heart tightened in my chest.

This? This was what I was supposed to do? To get my heart broken so fast with a critically ill kitten? I tried not to let my tears land on her. *Please,* I kept thinking. *Please.*

I watched her breathe, listened to her purr. *Don't let her die. I don't even know her yet. Please.*

The vet agreed that she was seriously ill. She was dehydrated and needed IV fluids at the very least. My tiny little not-a-penguin kitten was admitted to the hospital, and I left with an empty crate.

When I got home, I was finally able to reach the tech who set up the adoption. She suggested that I bring both kittens back to the clinic—once the girl kitten was stable enough to travel—and there they would nurse the little one back to health. She thought having her brother to keep her company would help her recover.

After discussing the plan with the veterinarian at the emergency vet, I tucked my healthy still-unnamed little masked kitten into the crate, collected my ill baby, and brought them both to the clinic.

Over the next several days, they tended to my sick kitten and brought her back to health. She had lost so much weight during her illness, it was touch and go for a while. But because I had moved quickly, and she got the care she needed—and because she was a fighter—she survived.

After four days, she was well enough to come home.

On the way to the vet to pick them up, I was inspired. The male cat had a mask that reminded me of Calvin, from the comic strip *Calvin and Hobbes.* Calvin would dress up as a character he called Stupendous Man, with a mask and cape. Our boy kitten had black along his back, which could easily serve as a cape. He was an amusing little superhero—with superpowers that helped heal his sister. He was Calvin.

I had become increasingly unhappy with Claire as a name for our thin girl. It felt unlucky. It seemed like it was the name of the sick kitten as opposed to the now healthier and quite energetic ball of fluff I saw when I picked up my two babies at the vet's office. She stalked a cotton ball and then pounced on it like a miniature lion. Maybe I could call her Elsa, like the lioness from one of my favorite books as a young girl, *Born Free*. Elsa was raised by humans after being orphaned when she was just weeks old; she survived to become the first lion raised by people and successfully released to the wild. She was a strong, loving character. But it still didn't seem quite right.

When I had first considered Claire, I had looked the name up online. Claire—or more specifically *clair*—means "light" in French. I couldn't quite drop the name Claire because the kitten lived through her illness under that name. But what if I took off the "e" in Claire so it wasn't exactly her hospital name, but more about the idea of light?

As I was checking out at the vet's office, the woman behind the counter looked up at me. "Did you decide on names for them?"

I smiled. "The boy is Calvin. And the little girl is Elsa Clair."

Today, Calvin (who is known on Instagram as Calvin Tiberius Katz, the Most Interesting Cat in the World) is my constant buddy, a sidekick who likes to ride on my shoulder and bring me toys as gifts. Elsa Clair is my muse—or should I say "mews"—who sleeps in a cat bed on my desk, every now and again awakening to take a short stroll to my lap to exchange pets for purrs. I also have a window perch just above my work area, where Elsa Clair lounges on a sunny day, her tail slowly swishing back and forth, providing a centering and calming focus for me when I need inspiration.

The wrong kittens turned out to be the right kittens after all.

8

A Tug at My Heart

Kathrine Diedre Smith

Years ago, I was asked to help feed a feral cat colony. As a lifelong animal lover, I have maintained a particularly strong relationship with cats ever since I was six years of age when I rescued and adopted my first cat, Cindy.

An elderly woman who fed numerous feral cat colonies in our area heard about me and said she needed help. So we met, and I agreed to take over the nightly feeding responsibilities for one active feral cat colony, and in addition I would often drive the woman's detailed route to feed over a hundred other cats throughout our community. It was a daunting task, which took a minimum of two hours every night, just to drive and deliver food and water to each location. The feral cat colony I inherited was located just over a mile from my home. I was told not to interact with the colony or the cats, just to dump food on the ground and drive away. However, I'm not exactly a "dump and go" kind of person. I am more of a relationship and trust-building person, even with cats. The colony had never been treated as having a partnership with a human. They only had each other, and even that didn't always work out well for them.

The bigger and bolder kitties would often come up to eat, while the smaller and more timid cats would remain hidden and only venture up later to lick up any leftovers off the ground, if they were lucky enough to find any. There was illness and rapid turnover in the colony. Even though the previous caretaker did participate in TNR (trap, neuter, release), there was a high incidence of cats vanishing or being euthanized due to illness. I wanted to change that.

One night while out feeding, I saw an adult cat with four very young kittens. I assumed the adult was their mother, but something seemed out of place. I began bringing them kitten food, serving them in bowls, and spending more time with the colony, keeping some distance in order for them to feel comfortable, but still allowing me to observe the behavior and dynamics of the colony. The kittens would always come up, but their guardian would not. Stealthy and elusive, the adult cat would stay back, hidden in the bushes, constantly fixing translucent green eyes on me. It was almost a month later that I realized the kittens' caretaker was actually a male—an intact male cat who was acting as both guardian and protector for the four young kittens. He was obviously quite special, but totally distrustful of humans.

I actively trapped cats in that colony for TNR, but the elusive male cat would not go anywhere near a trap. No matter how tasty the bait or foolproof the trap, he wouldn't go near it. Even when I wasn't there. This feral tomcat wasn't particularly large, more of a medium build. He was primarily white, with rather large splashes of solid gray on his back and sides, a solid white chest and belly, and two adorable gray patches covering his ears. Although he was rather average in stature and had no stripes, this boy had the heart of a tiger! The first time I heard him speak, he had the most soul-fully deep baritone voice I had ever heard, and he meowed like he was singing to his people—or the colony, if not to the world. His cries struck me to my core, and I couldn't help but be moved by him. No matter how hard I tried, I could never get close to this elusive boy with the deep soulful voice. And he would never get anywhere near a trap.

Late one night in March, when we were experiencing one of the rainiest months here on record, I went out to feed the colonies. In addition to my own colony, I had been asked to feed some other feral cat colonies outside my area, because roads were flooded and impassible for small vehicles, and I drive a tall pickup truck. While I was out feeding, I got out of my truck at each location to set up multiple feeding stations on higher ground, checking to see if the feral kitties were okay. Just as I was getting ready to leave and had my hand on the door to open my truck, I heard a very weak, mournful cry. I turned around and peered in the dark, calling out in the rain. I heard his cries again; it was the elusive boy from my other colony! But that other colony was several miles away. I was shocked. What was he doing here?

Ferals often seek shelter in storm drains. Apparently, he had been washed down a storm sewer drain and was swept away underground through a series of drainage pipes by the flooding rainwater. For miles. It was a miracle that he was alive. And especially that he found me. I grabbed a flashlight and quickly ventured in the direction of his voice. Slowly and rather unsteadily, he climbed out of the storm sewer pipe and sort of lay there. He was soaking wet and worn out. I went to him and touched him gently, wanting to give him comfort. He let me. I knelt beside him for a while, just talking to him and letting him know he was going to be okay. He looked up at me and locked eyes with mine. I knew I needed to get him back to his colony. But I had no carrier or crate, nothing to put him in. I could hear more thunder in the distance and knew my time with him out in the open was limited.

I put my hands around the cat and started to lift, then felt a very low, rumbling growl. The kind that gets your attention because the cat is serious. Well, what do I do now? It was at that moment that I had a conversation with this boy. I told him I was there for him, to help him and bring him home. But in order for me to help, I told him that I needed his help too. I needed him to work with me, so that we could get him home. Then I tried lifting him up again, and this time he let me. This boy who had never allowed human hands anywhere near him was letting me carry him to my truck!

Once I got there, I thought, now what? Do I let go of him and hope he doesn't become a loose cannon in my truck, or do I hold him and hope he doesn't bite and try to tear me up? I figured that if I wanted his trust, then I needed to give him my trust as well. So I slowly loaded myself and him in the truck and kept him on my lap. I could feel how cold he was, and his soaked body pressed into my leg, with my wet blue jeans acting as the only buffer for his sharp claws, as he held on dearly to my right thigh for comfort and stability. It was at that moment that I named him Tug, because he was clearly tugging at my heart.

I waited awhile with him in my lap, wondering how in the world I would start my truck. Tug was the most street-smart kitty I knew, and the sound of a vehicle would always send him running away. Only this time, he was captive. So was I. All I knew to do was to keep talking to Tug in a calm, reassuring voice. I told him how much I loved him and that his family missed him. I told him how beautiful he was, even though he was totally disheveled and looked like a drowned rat. But he was my Tug, and I just knew that somehow we would get through this. Together. I felt him dig his claws deeply through my blue jeans and into my leg, and I thought, *Lord, what did I get myself into?*

Suddenly, I felt his sharp claws retract. Then I felt his claws back in my leg again, like in slow motion, intensifying then retracting over and over again. He was kneading, or as many cat lovers say, he was making bread on me. I started to weep. Somehow, we both knew everything was going to be okay. I put my key in the ignition and started the truck. I felt him dig his front claws in a little deeper, but not his back ones. He softened his grip but continued holding on to me and seemed ready to go. I took the truck out of neutral and slowly moved forward. I prayed for no traffic, no sudden movement, and that we would both get back to Tug's home in one piece, with no incidents. We did!

When we got back to his home turf, I parked the truck and we just sat there for a while. I dried Tug off with my jacket and kept talking to him. I felt a vibration from his throat, but this time it was a gentle purr. We must have sat there in my truck for another hour. By this time, another round of rain had passed, and the ominous weather began to clear. I opened the door to my truck and carried Tug out. He was so calm and relaxed now, and he let me place him back on familiar soil, albeit a bit damp. Then, as he stepped away, he looked over his shoulder at me, like he was saying, "Thanks for believing in me," and he slipped into the protective covering of his favorite thick evergreen shrubs.

The next morning when I went out to check on the colony, Tug came running up to greet me, tail up in the air, followed by his troop of adoring adolescent kittens! From that moment on, our connection of love and trust grew. A month later, when

haiku

stray cat in back yard
watches humans through windows
decides this is home

I knew that Tug was healthy and strong enough to withstand surgery, I scheduled him to be neutered and fully vetted. When I went out to his colony the night before his surgery and called for him, Tug came running up to me, just as he did every night after his storm sewer rescue.

This time, I picked Tug up and calmly placed him inside an enclosed travel crate, with no growling and no incidents whatsoever. He had never been in a crate before, but he handled it beautifully. He was my copilot, and I was his guardian.

With Tug, there was never a need for a trap again. Besides, traps don't work for some kitties. What does work is earning their trust and allowing someone special to tug at your heart.

9

Texas Big Box Stray to Minnesota Family Cat

Mary Tan

I woke up bright and early that March day, exhausted after a long week of bringing puppies to area television stations at the crack of dawn. As the public relations manager at Animal Humane Society (AHS) in Minnesota's Twin Cities of Minneapolis and Saint Paul, I had pitched the idea of featuring adoptable puppies on morning news shows for National Puppy Day. Our local stations turned this event into a weeklong celebration, much to the delight of their audiences.

It was a rewarding week, but today was the day I was looking forward to. The American Society for Prevention of Cruelty to Animals (ASPCA) was funding a flight that would bring more than a hundred cats, several dozen dogs, and thirteen pigs to Minnesota from the Humane Society of North Texas in Fort Worth. The flight was organized by Wings of Rescue, a California nonprofit that flies homeless animals from states where shelters are overcrowded to communities with a greater capacity for adoption. My shelter would take in about half of the dogs and cats, and two other Minnesota rescue groups, Feline Rescue and Ruff Start Rescue, would take in the rest. The 150-pound potbellied pigs went to the Dubuque Humane Society in Iowa.

I got to the small airport an hour early, just in case the flight landed ahead of schedule. Soon staff and volunteers from the other animal rescue organizations arrived, along with a few members of the media I had invited. Everyone waited, eyes sparkling with excitement and anticipation.

The Wings of Rescue plane finally arrived and taxied to where we were waiting. It was a midsized cargo jet with just three seats— for the pilot, copilot, and a Wings of Rescue volunteer. The rest of the space was devoted to kennels and crates for animals who would soon find second chances in a new state.

As soon as the cargo door opened, the sights, sounds, and smells of the animals filled the air. The dogs barked with excitement while the cats and kittens meowed at the unknown. The animals were safely housed in kennels of various sizes—big dogs and pigs in huge crates while petite cats sat cozily in small carriers. There were multiple momma cats with their tiny mewing kittens in tow, each family in its own crate.

Nearly twenty of us there to help unload the plane whooped with joy and enthusiasm at the first glimpse of those furry faces. It was an emotional high for everyone. After the exuberance subsided, we worked quickly to get the animals unloaded. That night, with great satisfaction for everyone involved, the Texas cats, dogs, and pigs spent their first night in the Midwest—safe and sound in their new shelters and foster homes.

I went to bed early that night, but I couldn't fall asleep even though I was exhausted. I picked up my phone and started watching local news coverage of the event. Then on a whim of curiosity, I went on Facebook to read what the Humane Society of North Texas had posted about the event from their end. That's when I stumbled upon the emotional posts Texas foster families had written about the animals they'd been caring for who just arrived in Minnesota. They knew the animals were going to a good place, but it didn't make saying good-bye any easier. They missed their cats and dogs dearly. I quickly posted a message saying that the animals had arrived safely in Minnesota.

Within moments, I received a direct message from Jessica Tovar, a foster volunteer who had put a momma cat and her babies on the flight.

Mary,

I work at a home improvement store in Fort Worth where I rescued a momma cat named Checkers along with her babies. The night manager at my job wanted them put down. I was not going to allow that to happen and took them home. Fortunately, my husband and I had recently moved into our first house and had space to foster them, with the help of the Humane Society of North Texas. After we took them in, we were able to litterbox train them and get them comfortable with humans. We wanted to keep them, but we already have four cats. Giving them up to the shelter after getting close to them was the hardest thing. After lots of tears, we surrendered them, but we can't stop feeling sad. I don't think I'll be able to forget the look Checkers gave me as I drove her and her kittens to the shelter. I feel as if she thought we were going to be her new family. I would like to know how she is doing.

*As I'm writing this, I'm bawling my eyes out wondering
if they are scared or doing okay.*

My mind started racing. Which momma was Checkers? I remembered seeing a few sets of feline families earlier that day. Then the emotional thought of giving up a little family like this hit me. I would be in tears too if I were in the same situation, so I wrote Jessica back immediately saying I would try to honor her request and provide an update on Checkers and her kittens. We continued messaging each other into the wee hours of the night, and I got more information about Checkers.

The next morning, I got to work early to inquire about Checkers. I was excited to learn that she and her babies were delivered safely to AHS. I ran downstairs to check on the sweet family. The tortoiseshell feline and her kittens were resting contentedly. The babies' paws twitched and mouths gently opened and closed as they dreamed. I didn't want to wake them so I quietly snapped some photos.

As I stopped to look at the sleeping momma, Checkers must have sensed I was there as she opened her eyes. I quietly opened the cage door and gave her some pets as her young kittens slept. I couldn't believe this tiny girl had been living in a home improvement store in Texas up until a few weeks ago. I gave her some chin scratches and then sent the photos off to Jessica.

Checkers was born in July of 2017 with her sister Pinwheel (Penny) and brother Butters. The three lived in the outdoor garden center of a huge home improvement store in Fort Worth, where college students Jessica Tovar and Jocelyn Rodriguez Ramirez worked part-time. Jessica and Jocelyn shared a love of cats and took it upon themselves to care for the furry threesome with the help of a few other coworkers. This litter was standoffish at first, but soon Penny and Butters became comfortable with people.

Butters was so affectionate that he began to sit at the counter as people checked out, and returning customers knew him by name. Butters eventually went home with an employee. Penny, who is now spayed, still lives at the store, where she can often be found reclining on lawn bags.

Checkers was a different story. She was wary of people and would run away if anyone got too close. Jocelyn and Jessica spent time during each shift working to tame and socialize Checkers.

Their efforts paid off. Soon the young kitty was following them everywhere! When Jocelyn was transferred to another area of the store, she continued to visit Checkers and bring her treats. In the summer of 2018, Checkers figured out how to activate the motion sensors on the store's automatic sliding doors so she could come in and escape the sizzling Texas heat. From that point on, the wayward cat became Jocelyn's shadow, following her inside the store and throughout the electrical department, demanding pets and belly rubs while Jocelyn restocked light bulbs and extension cords.

Mundane work activities became more entertaining with Checkers. Jocelyn gave her boxes to play and nap in. One day she entertained Checkers by folding electrical tape together and cutting fringe into it. Jocelyn dangled it in front of Checkers and suddenly got to see the carefree side of this cat. From that point on, Jocelyn attached the dangling electrical tape to her cart so Checkers would always follow.

Customers would often be surprised to see Checkers at the busy warehouse store. It was such a rough place for a shy kitty to be playful. Checkers still didn't trust strangers, and Jocelyn often warned customers the cat might scratch them if they were too forward with her.

In December of 2018, store employees noticed the tortoiseshell kitty was gaining weight. It soon became clear she was pregnant. The store's managers had already threatened to throw the resident felines out of the store. News of a new litter would not be taken well, and Jocelyn and Jessica feared for the worst since they had struggled to place past litters of kittens.

On February 8, 2019, Checkers gave birth to four kittens at the store. At first, Jessica and Jocelyn couldn't find the babies. After looking high and low all over the store, they found them secluded in flower pots outside the garden center. The healthy kittens grew and began to venture out on their own. That's when management found them and told the employees the kittens were to be euthanized.

Upon hearing this, Jessica vowed to protect these babies and went to look for them. They were not by the flower pots as they usually were. She searched and searched and found the kittens alone next to the store's trash compactor. She grabbed them and took them home that day.

Jessica knew she couldn't separate the kittens from their mother. She called Jocelyn and the two devised a plan to trap the wayward momma. Expecting a long night, they prepared a large crate with plenty of blankets, treats, and wet, delicious cat food. They went to the store with gear in tow and set it down next to the outside garden registers where Checkers often would hang out. Much to their shock, the tortie walked into the crate within minutes! Both Jessica and Jocelyn laughed at their extensive preparation for what turned out to be a relatively easy task.

Checkers and her kittens were reunited at Jessica's house that day, and Momma was thrilled to see her babies. But now they had a new challenge: neither of them had the resources to care for five cats. They decided to reach out to local animal organizations for help.

haiku

shelter cat's eyes say:
rescue me and I promise
I'll rescue you back

That afternoon Jocelyn and Jessica went to the Humane Society of North Texas to see if Checkers and her babies could be
rehomed through them. They brought the happy family along,
hoping for the best.

Staff at the Texas shelter sadly explained that, due to limited
space, they had to prioritize animals who would make great house
pets. If Checkers was feral, she and her kittens would have to be
euthanized. The two cat rescuers knew they couldn't let that happen. They went back to their car and immediately started calling
every animal rescue organization in the area.

A few minutes later, the same staff member came out to their
car and told them there might be another option. There was going
to be a flight where more than a hundred animals would go to less
crowded shelters in Minnesota. If Checkers was a good candidate
for the flight, she and her babies could find loving homes 940 miles
to the north.

Jessica and Jocelyn went back inside with Checkers and her
litter in tow. During the exam, Checkers was on her best behavior.
It seemed like the young tortie knew she needed to be perfectly
behaved to save herself and her kittens. Shelter staff agreed the
sweet momma cat and kittens were fit for the trip, but it wasn't
for another week. Jessica and Jocelyn agreed to care for the family
until then, thrilled they could have a little more time with their
favorite kitties.

The next week went quickly. Jessica and Jocelyn took shifts
spending time with Checkers and the babies. Jessica was with
them in the morning and Jocelyn would visit in the afternoon.
The kittens grew steadily, and Checkers was becoming more and
more friendly. They were also relieved Checkers used the litterbox
on a regular basis.

The day before the flight, Jocelyn spent her final afternoon with
Checkers. Jocelyn cried and explained to the little feline family

that they were loved, valued, and would be deeply missed. She also felt anxious knowing that there were no guarantees the future shelter would not euthanize Checkers for being too feral. Jocelyn knew she had no choice but to hope for the best. She said one last prayer, reassured the animals, said good-bye, and cried the rest of the way home.

The next day Jessica had the difficult duty of taking Checkers and the kittens to the shelter for their flight to Minnesota. She too found the good-bye emotionally unbearable. Jessica told me that at one point Checkers put her paw on her arm and gave a look as if to say: "Why are you abandoning us?" It was too much, and Jessica broke into tears. After their final good-bye, Jessica left, full of sadness, yet hopeful for Checkers and her babies.

After their arrival at my shelter, I paid particular attention to Checkers, visiting her and the babies in their kennel every day. I felt it was my duty to watch over them for Jessica and Jocelyn. Eventually, our veterinary staff determined the kittens were officially weaned. Checkers would make her debut in our adoption center while the kittens went to a foster home until they were big enough to be spayed or neutered.

After the kittens went to a foster volunteer, Checkers was placed in one of our colony rooms, a large space where adopters can interact and play with available felines. Checkers loved to climb the cat trees in the room and cuddle with the other kitties, but her stay would be very temporary.

Within a few days, the Green family came to the shelter in search of the perfect cat. Susan Green, along with her granddaughters Natalie and Ellie, had recently lost a feline due to illness. They decided it was time to look for a new companion for their remaining kitty, Teddy.

Susan's ten-year-old granddaughter Ellie led the search, playing with and looking at every cat she could see and touch. From a distance, she spotted Checkers sitting on a ledge in her colony room. The little girl walked into the room, gave the kitty a look over, and proclaimed, "Grandma, that's the one. You have to have her." The three visited with Checkers in a private room and Susan agreed, "Yes, she's the one."

Safe and loved in her new home, Checkers has blossomed into the perfect cat. She loves to curl up with Teddy and has favorite spots on the Green family's comfy furniture. Her kittens quickly found new homes too. Being so cute, almost all were adopted the same day they were put on the adoption floor.

Back in Texas, Jocelyn graduated from college and is pursuing a career in finance. Jessica is still in school and hopes to become an accountant in the near future. Both say they'll continue their work helping felines, fostering stray cats and any kittens who come their way.

Checkers is just one of thousands of cats my animal shelter takes in each year. I am so proud we help not only cats in Minnesota, but cats in communities across the nation through animal transport. Long ago I realized only people can make life better for animals. I am thankful for Jessica and Jocelyn and countless others who work together, near and far, to help these animals. Together we can make sure every animal is loved and cared for.

10

The Love of Her Life

Tracy Crump

Darkness surrounded me when I walked out of the small ceramics shop where I worked part-time to make a little Christmas money. The cold December wind sliced through my coat, and I strained to see my car in the unlit parking lot.

Then I heard it.

A faint mew came from somewhere under the closest car. I leaned down and saw the merest glint of light shining off two beautiful green eyes. Oh no. Not again. We already had two hefty male cats at home, both saved from life on the streets. Plus a dog. We didn't need another pet. But what else could I do? I reached under and pulled out a solid black kitten, no more than six or seven weeks old. She immediately nestled herself into my arms.

When I got home with the tiny fur ball, my husband, Stan, rolled his eyes but didn't say a word. She looked up at him and meowed pitifully until he pulled out a can of cat food and put a dish of it on the floor. She cleaned the plate, rubbed against his leg, and went straight to the litterbox to do her business. What a good girl! She soon curled up on an old blanket and fell asleep.

We made a feeble attempt to find our newest charge another home, but it was too late. Within a few days, she'd charmed her way into our hearts and into our family. We named her Beth. Whether she started life malnourished or just inherited delicate genes, our little cat remained just that—a little cat.

At a mere six pounds, Beth was by far the smallest of our three felines. Though never aggressive, she could hold her own against the boys, one of which was almost three times her size. When Beth got ready to eat, she muscled her way to the food bowl. If either of the other cats challenged her, she hissed in their face. Surprisingly, they would back down. I enjoyed having a female ally in our male-dominated household, and we spent long evenings snuggled in my quilted sleep sack while I read and Beth snoozed. We became the best of friends.

But Stan was the love of her life.

Beth would follow Stan around the house until he sat down. Then she'd jump into his lap and stretch her full length to nuzzle his neck. Rubbing her face back and forth on his chin, she marked Stan as hers and hers alone, but I didn't mind. Stan sat and petted her for hours while watching soccer games or a movie. She didn't even seem to notice if he rubbed her fur backward, something that drove the other cats crazy.

More than cuddling on the couch, Beth enjoyed game time. Our cats loved to play "flashlight." We'd close the blinds, and they would chase the light around the room, over the furniture, and up the walls—wherever Stan shined it. Our house lost a bit of its value from this game, but none of the cats ever tired of it.

However, one game originated with Beth and became hers alone. When Stan would pop the plastic safety ring off a new gallon of milk, she would come running. Beth didn't care a thing about milk, but she loved to bat the ring around the kitchen floor until it disappeared beneath an appliance. At least a hundred plastic rings took up residence with the dust bunnies under our fridge.

No matter what Stan did, his little friend was never far away. Beth couldn't stand to be separated from him for long. One morning, Stan pulled down the attic stairs to move some items up for storage. He climbed the ladderlike steps, and I stood at the bottom handing up boxes while Beth paced back and forth like a miniature panther. Each time Stan disappeared from the attic opening to carry something to a far corner, she yowled until he came back into sight. Finally, we finished moving everything up, and Stan remained in the attic for several minutes rearranging boxes. I went to the bedroom to fold clothes, glad Beth had calmed down at last. When Stan came down, he closed the stairs and went on to the next project.

That afternoon, Stan pulled the ring from a milk jug and waited for Beth to show up. But she didn't.

"Huh," he said. "Maybe she's taking a catnap."

A little while later, we darkened the living room for a game of flashlight. Two cats bounded in. Still no Beth. Now we knew something was wrong. We began searching under beds, in the laundry basket, around the plants, in all the places she normally napped. When we neared the attic opening, we heard a faint sound. Could it be? Stan pulled down the stairs, and a cat dropped into his arms.

Beth had climbed ten steps—spread far enough apart she could barely reach from one to the next—just to be near her beloved. It may not seem like a superhuman feat, but it was quite a challenge for our pint-sized cat. I had no doubt she thought danger lurked in the attic and she had to brave the unknown to rescue Stan. Sometimes love gives us courage to do things we would otherwise think impossible.

71

It broke my heart to think of Beth creeping along the dark rafters, searching for her sweetheart, but her act of selfless love left us with an example we could apply to our own lives. Whenever I found myself sinking into a "me first" mentality, I thought of Beth and her daring feat and became inspired to overcome any hurdle to help those I loved.

What would we have missed had I not pulled a shivering black kitten from under a car in a dark parking lot? Life might have been easier without three cats, but just like a third child, that last addition brought us so much joy. Stan was the love of Beth's life, but her love multiplied and spilled over to enrich our home more than we could ever have envisioned.

11

The Story of Harry and Hermione

Debbie De Louise

I first saw Harry and Hermione on a cool and sunny Sunday afternoon in late October. It was the second visit for my thirteen-year-old daughter and me to the newly opened Shabby Tabby Cat Café on Long Island. Since we'd said good-bye to our seventeen-year-old Siamese, Oliver, when he'd succumbed to kidney disease nearly a year ago, we'd started considering adopting another cat. Holly had found one she was interested in on our previous visit to the cat café, but it hadn't worked out because the kitten had already been claimed. Because she'd been so disappointed, I'd assured her that we would keep looking until she found the cat that was meant for her.

This time, among the cats and kittens who greeted visitors, Holly spotted a black kitten by the Halloween-decorated windows. He wore a red bow tie with a tag that read "Harry." She began to play with him with a cat teaser the café supplied and was impressed with how friendly he was and how high he could jump. While she was playing with Harry, I noticed another kitten with the most beautiful pattern of fur in shades of peach, gray, and white. She was walking around with a proud stance, head and tail held high, near an empty play tent that displayed a sign that read "FIV positive kittens. Don't be afraid. They aren't contagious." I'd heard of FIV (feline immunodeficiency virus) but wasn't too familiar with the disease.

After playing with Harry for a while, Holly announced that she had fallen in love with him. I could see why. He was a playful fellow who seemed affectionate and bright although a bit quiet. His golden eyes held a hint of a shy and sweet nature. When I asked if he was available, I was told he was but that he couldn't be separated from his sister, Hermione, the proud dilute-shaded calico I'd noticed strutting around. My husband had only agreed to adopting one cat because we still had Stripey, our ten-year-old cat, at home. But I felt as if the pair was meant for us.

Holly had always wanted a black cat, and although I'd had many cats all my life, I'd never had a calico. I am a writer of mysteries, and ironically, I'd just published the fourth book of my Cobble Cove cozy mystery series, *Love on the Rocks*, which introduced a calico kitten into the fictional town. As a cat lover, author, and also a member of the Cat Writers' Association, I enjoyed writing about cats and giving them roles in my books. My series already had a Siamese, a library cat named Sneaky who'd been based on our Oliver. The idea of introducing a calico kitten into the new novel came from a character-naming contest among my readers. The winner, a fellow librarian, had sent a photo of her calico cat along with her name.

When I learned that Harry and Hermione were the kittens who were kept in the cat tent with the FIV-positive sign, I had some concerns. However, the cat café owner explained to us that some kittens whose mothers are infected with FIV will test positive until their immune systems are mature. She informed us that if we adopted Harry and Hermione, the Golden Paw Society, the shelter from which they came, would pay for the retest when they were six months old. If the kittens remained positive, they could still lead long and healthy lives as long as they were kept indoors and saw a vet regularly. She also said that if the cats had FIV, there was only a slim chance that they would infect our other cat unless Stripey received a deep bite from one of them.

I was feeling more at ease as I watched the kittens respond to my daughter with deep purrs. I called my husband, and although he wasn't thrilled about adopting two kittens, he finally agreed. He knew how much Holly wanted another cat and shared my feelings that it would be nice for her to learn how to care for and raise kittens, as she'd been too young for that experience with our other cats. I completed the adoption forms. We picked the kittens up on Wednesday night, October 24, which happened to be Holly's birthday.

Holly kept the kittens in her room initially until Stripey could adjust to having two new felines in the house. We knew they were ready for an introduction when Hermione started sticking her white paws under the door and playing "pawsy" with Stripey. We then began to introduce them for short periods until Stripey stopped hissing at them and seemed to welcome the company of kittens that brought new toys and more activity into the house.

Harry and Hermione both retested negative for FIV. While waiting for the results, I knew that no matter what, we would keep and love the precious additions to our household. I felt that they'd eased the pain of our family's loss of Oliver and also of my mother, who'd passed away a few months before we adopted the kittens.

I'm sure there are people who would think twice about bringing FIV-positive kittens into their homes, because I have to admit that I did. Yet there are those who foster and adopt kittens and cats with disabilities, those missing limbs or who have been abused or injured in accidents. When fate steps in and brings a cat or cats into your life, you can't turn your back. I'm glad I didn't.

Harry and Hermione are now healthy and beautiful cats. Harry has overcome his shyness and is quite vocal. He loves to play and jumps even higher to catch his favorite cat teaser. Hermione is pretty and sweet. She likes high places and soft blankets and is just as proud of herself as when I first laid eyes on her. Stripey has adjusted to them, and the three often play together. Holly is even more in love with them since she's watched them grow. I'm convinced that they were meant for us, and we were meant for them.

12

Spartacus the Big Red Cat

Kristin Billerbeck

After a traumatic change in circumstances, my teenage daughter and I were sharing a six-hundred-square-foot, one-bedroom apartment. When we left our house, we could not keep our dog. My daughter, being a huge pet person, longed for a cat to cuddle and make her feel safe. I came up with a thousand reasons why we could not have a cat.

The apartment is too small.

I'm not really a cat person.

I'm deathly allergic to cat hair.

None of these excuses were worthy against a fifteen-year-old girl who needed something to call her own. So I promised to go to the shelter "just to look." It would give her a few moments with some kittens and she'd leave happy.

"We're just looking," I reminded my daughter before we went inside. "You understand?"

She nodded excitedly as we entered the shelter. Now, these shelters know exactly what they're doing. You're locked in this cramped room with a bevy of little furry beauties and all their frenzied cat energy. They're all mewling and snuggling their soft, tender heads into the crook of your arms, legs—whatever is available to them. I defy even the coldest heart to leave that room without a kitty.

"I've never had a cat," I said as a protective stance against my softening heart. "I don't know what to do with one."

"I'll take care of it, Mommy. I promise!"

"You said that about the dog."

"But I'm not a dog person," my daughter reminded me. "I always said I wanted a cat."

Well, that was true, I reasoned.

Randy was a tiny white kitten with an orange head and tail. His paws were too big for his scrawny body, and he felt like the softest mink stole from your grandmother's closet. My daughter sat calmly for nearly an hour with Randy roosted in her lap, and I thought, *This is just what she needs. This will help her through these tough times.*

So, after one hundred dollars in supplies and more paperwork than I had filled out to take any of my four children home, Randy was ours. We took him home, where he hid under a bed for two days.

"This is it?" I asked Elle. "Having a cat means buying expensive food and litter so the cat can live hidden away and never come out?"

"You have to give them time to warm up. He'll come out eventually."

In the meantime, my son was home from Marine boot camp and he, being in warrior mode, changed the name of Randy to something more "manly"—Spartacus. Little did I know how accurate that name would grow to be. Spartacus, our little munchkin kitten, turned out to be a Turkish Van. Now, if like me, you have no idea what that means, that means Spartacus was going to grow. And grow. And grow.

Turkish Vans are enormous cats—and they like water. So much so that if you left the bathroom door open a crack when you were in the bathtub, Spartacus would nudge it open and promptly hop on top of you—all eighteen pounds of him!

The tiny apartment could not contain Spartacus. Our dream of having a contented "apartment kitty" quickly went by the wayside, and we had to let him outside. He had the loudest meow I'd ever heard and he made his demands clear. He had so much energy from early on. He would climb my daughter's boho-chic tapestry on the wall and hang there like Spider-man. Until he got too large to "fly" and his claws grabbed on for dear life as the material shredded into two pieces and dropped Spartacus on the carpet.

Turkish Vans are also rabid hunters. Since we lived in a building with neighbors for whom it's cultural to leave your shoes outside, that meant sometimes the neighbors might get a live mouse curled up in their loafer as a "gift." One time, Spartacus was outside on the second-story porch meowing so loud, it was like a toddler wailing for all to witness my bad cat parenting. I opened the door, and Spartacus just stared at me but wouldn't step foot in the door. Slowly, I turned my head to the doorjamb and nearly jumped out of my skin when I saw a mouse at eye level as he clutched the frame for dear life.

I screamed and shut the door. My daughter Elle was horrified. "Mom, he'll hurt the mouse."

"He probably will," I agreed. *The circle of life, baby.*

My daughter grabbed a pillow, wrapped it in a plastic bag, and put it outside so the mouse could fall on the pillow. She then grabbed Spartacus and brought him inside, where he continued meowing obnoxiously for an hour. I kept checking the peephole and watched that mouse go in and out of my neighbors' shoes until it finally made its way downstairs. I breathed a sigh of relief but still feared the worst if I let Spartacus outside again.

At this time, my son was a full-fledged Marine serving in Okinawa. He was FaceTiming us from his base when he saw the cat in the background. "What are you feeding that thing? It's giant! It's like a mountain lion now."

As Spartacus got bigger, so did the gifts he brought us. Once he brought us a healthy, robust rat. I wasn't home at the time, and my daughter, ever the animal lover, thought it would be a good idea to put on plastic gloves and "rescue" the rat. That ended in a bite through the rubber gloves and a trip to the ER. Spartacus was quickly getting on my nerves.

A few days later, my daughter was having a slumber party on the living room floor, and at 5:30 a.m., the cat started meowing loudly to come in the apartment. Elle never thought to check Spartacus first and opened the door widely. The live mouse in Spartacus's mouth dropped and skittered across the sleeping bags and disappeared under the refrigerator.

The next day, I left the patio door open so we could lose our little friend, but that mouse—that bold, unnerving little rodent—ended up in my daughter's bed the next night. He stared her right in the face like they were sharing good times—a slumber party of their own. I ran up with a broom and chased it through the apartment until it disappeared again under the fridge.

This was not how I pictured having a cat. Maybe I'd romanticized it a bit, this whole idea of an emotional support animal, but I never thought I'd be chasing vermin through my living room in the middle of the night while my daughter cracked up at my "overreaction."

"Do you know how many diseases those things carry? This is dangerous!"

Elle shrugged. "Eh, we'll survive."

Spartacus needed more space—more space without the handy "drive-thru" of an apartment garbage collection site. Through many tears, we made the hard decision to move him to a home a few blocks away, and Elle visited daily. It broke my heart that we didn't have the house for the cat. I wanted my daughter to have her pet where he belonged—with her.

Today, it's many years later, and Elle has her cat back in her arms permanently. She has moved to the country, and Spartacus has room to roam. He is a regal, incredible feline who could model for any cat product. He still has silky soft, downy fur and a strong need to cuddle. He sleeps in the crook of my daughter's neck and purrs his appreciation nightly. He's lost a little energy and now spends much less time outdoors.

I love this cat for all his feline ways, for all the warmth, giggles, and crazy scenarios that helped us appreciate our life's changes. I love him mostly for the way he showed me that my daughter is indeed a cat person. And what do you know? So am I.

13

It Happened at Big Lots

Deborah Camp

So there I was, shopping at the Big Lots store in Millington, Tennessee, minding my own business. I'd just finished attending the Navy College graduation ceremony, and in the split second before turning my car toward the highway heading home, I swung in the opposite direction, acting on a sudden impulse. Although the clouds threatened a steamy late-spring thunderstorm, I decided to dash into the shopping center to swoop up some cans of premium cat food—always a bargain at this particular outlet.

I filled my cart and rolled toward the checkout. Turning the corner at the end of the aisle, I almost bumped into a stocky, ponytailed gal who was an employee at the store. Surveying the contents of my cart, she observed in a country drawl, "Looks like you got you some cats at home." *Well, that's pretty obvious*, I thought.

I smiled brightly and agreed. "Yeah, we're down to just three now. Y'all got some good prices on cat food here!" I continued toward the counter, anxious to get home and out of my stuffy, dressed-up-for-graduation clothes.

"Come here. I wanna show you something." She beckoned me to follow. "It's back yonder in the break room."

What on *earth*? The girl seemed earnestly intent on my seeing whatever was at the back of the store. Was there a stash of premium food that hadn't yet made its way to the shelves?

I followed her into the fluorescent-lit room, and she pointed to a large cardboard box in the corner. I peered into it, and looking back up at me was a tiny yellow kitten, surely no more than six weeks old. He mewed plaintively. *Oh no you don't*, I thought. I must have the word *sucker* plastered all over me, but I was not taking home a new cat today. Attrition had thinned down our furry herd over the years, but after Yellow Man's passing in February, a new calm had settled comfortably over the remaining three cats and two dogs. After almost two decades of animals—at one point numbering thirteen mouths to feed and vet—five was a sane, reasonable number to look after.

But of course I made the mistake of inquiring about the plans for this small creature. As I listened to the employee explain how they found him at the back door that morning near the dumpster, soaked and shivering after a night of storms and pouring rain, I knew I'd be leaving the store with thirty-six cans of cat food and a kitten.

To my credit, I attempted to throw up some resistance. I interrogated the woman about any possible or even remote chance some other employee could take the cat home, or perhaps a local rescue group could be pressed into service. Every question was met with a negative response and firm head shake. "My brother, he kinda likes cats, but he's way up in Illinois," she offered with a shrug. "And you know the only shelter they got here, well, they got too many so they just put 'em down."

Oh no, I thought. "Well, let's saddle him up," I told her with resignation, wondering what my husband Michael was going to say. A smaller box was found and lined with a fluffy towel right off the home goods shelf, the $4.99 price tag still affixed. The employee transferred the open can of Friskies and a small plastic bowl of water into it. For good measure she included an unopened package of crunchy cat treats. I reached down and lifted the little guy from the box. He was feather light—hardly more than a pound. His tiny body was soft and warm, and his little heart beat wildly with fear. His blue eyes were wide and scared. *Okay, little dude, you're coming home with me.*

Several employees nodded their approval and high-fived each other as I made my way to the register. "God bless you!" exclaimed the assistant manager, a young tattooed fellow who said he would have adopted the kitten himself but couldn't because of allergies. Yeah, right. Another customer watching the commotion mumbled something about taking the cat if I didn't want him. *Where were you ten minutes ago?* I pretended not to hear her.

"Hey, y'all ought to gift me this cat food since I'm taking him off your hands," I suggested. They just laughed and rang up my total, excluding the swag they'd purloined from the shelves.

"What you gonna name him?" the country gal inquired.

"I'll call him Big Lots until I can come up with something."

Outside the sun beamed radiantly—all signs of rain had dissipated. It was as if heaven itself issued its stamp of approval on this tiny creature. Before I eased out of the shopping center with my precious cargo, I glanced down at little Big Lots, fully aware that life was getting ready to change significantly at our home in the cove. That settled calm would soon be ruffled by the energetic antics of this blue-eyed fluff ball. "All right, Big Lots—it's been fourteen years since we've had a kitten in the house. Are we going to have fun or what?" Big Lots blinked at me, yawned deeply, then curled into a tiny ball and slept all the way home.

An hour later I pulled into our driveway, wondering what everyone's reaction would be to this unexpected acquisition. I carried the mysterious box with its beat-up sides and packing tape streaming from its edges straight into the dining room and placed it on top of the long table.

"What's that?" Michael asked hesitantly, almost anticipating that whatever its contents, he was probably not going to approve.

"Have a look," I told him casually as I headed for the kitchen to put away the cans of cat food.

"Oh *no!*" I heard him exclaim from the dining room. "No, we can't! What happened . . . where? . . . no."

The sound of his voice trailed off as I made my way to the bedroom to get out of my sweaty pantsuit and pinching heels. By the time I'd returned, Michael had the kitten in the palm of his hand and was gently stroking his little body. I relayed the story of how I'd gone into the store to buy canned food and ended up rescuing this cat. Michael listened, and soon his frown smoothed as he held the kitten close to his face and rubbed its furry body with his nose. A short while later, he and the kitten were bonding in the sunroom.

Slowly and cautiously the other three cats appeared to take stock of the new arrival. What they saw did not impress them. There was some spitting and hissing, bushed-up tails, and dirty looks as Mali, Bummer, and Spot each weighed in with their opinions. If their expressions could have been translated, they would have read something like this: *What is this creature and who let him in? How soon will he be leaving—it won't be soon enough!*

Later the dogs got their turn. Old, arthritic Mooch leaned in for a friendly exploratory nuzzle and was immediately spurned as the kitten drew back in fear. Mojo, our goofy Aussie mix, tried his luck but was met with a flying, slapping paw. Introductions and adjustments were going to take some time.

By day 2, the kitten's placeholder name was changed to Bernie Uncle Ernie—or Bernie, for short. The name choice was easy, but we'd forgotten how chaotic kittens are and how they can turn daily life inside out. Within forty-eight hours, two humans, two dogs, and three cats were running on his busy schedule. More than a few times I wondered what new lessons God might be trying to teach me—teach all of us!

By the time Bernie was around six months old, he was the equivalent of a young, feisty juvenile. And while we knew this unruly phase would eventually run its course, our days were filled with the sounds of shrieks, growls, scuffling, hisses, snorts, and objects being broken. There were only four cats and two dogs in residence, but from the sound of scampering paws skittering across hardwood floors and the banging of flying fur bodies bumping against lamps, tables, and whatever wasn't anchored to the floor or ceiling, you'd have thought there were at least a dozen wild animals at large.

With human babies it's the terrible twos; with young cats it's the terrifying teens. Bernie was in his strutting prime—full of himself and proud of it. Like the popular seventh-grade class clown, he was high energy with no focus. His antics were mostly benign and often hilarious, but the problem was that our two female cats, Mali and Spot, were eighty and seventy-five in human years. Bummer, the only other male, was well into middle age at nine years, placing him around fifty-six.

haiku

we human beings
need our own purring cats to
show us how to love

Bernie was like a juvenile delinquent skateboarding through a retirement home. Mornings usually began with Bernie crashing our bed around 5:00 a.m., attacking our feet, jumping up and down, then moving from one of us to the other, biting our ears, licking our faces, or parking himself on our heads, where he'd dive his snout into our ears and commence with a long session of heavy breathing and purring. We finally resorted to barricading him in the den before bedtime, blocking off the hall leading to the bedroom.

The other cats weren't so fortunate. He was relentless in his pursuit to chase and torment them. He wasn't a bully—he was just full of pent-up energy and play. He needed somebody to tussle with, and that somebody was usually Bummer. Bernie's favorite game was to spring out of nowhere onto Bummer's back, dragging him down into a Brazilian jujitsu choke hold. His movements were versatile—complete with fancy footwork, impressive leg holds, and ground-fighting skills. Always surprised, Bummer would squawk with submission as he wrested himself free. Moments later Bernie would launch another attack, this time going for a guillotine choke or a Peruvian necktie with a single leg takedown. We finally had to keep a squirt gun handy to tame his annoying exuberance.

Eventually, Bernie outgrew his rambunctious teens, and at just over three years old, he's now mellowed into a fairly well-mannered gentleman. Our old man Mooch passed away two years ago, and all three geriatric cats who initially scorned Bernie's arrival have also crossed the Rainbow Bridge. Today, only Bernie and Mojo are still with us.

So what life lessons did this little Big Lots rescue teach us?

It reminded us once again that aging is a natural and mysterious part of life, not only for us but also for our companion animals. When we look at our cats, we see the stages of life accelerated.

The adorable kitten, the goofy toddler, the cocky teen, and the sleek adult transitioning into settled middle age. Bernie is now a thirtysomething feline in human years, and we've watched him move through each of these stages from an older, wiser perspective.

God knew the time was right for us to have Bernie. His unexpected appearance has brought us renewed joys and fresh adventures. It affords us further opportunities for joy, laughter, wonder, and observation. The successive losses of our other three elderly cats were painful but were somewhat softened by Bernie's ever-cheerful presence.

But most of all, we're reminded daily that just as we commit to each other our love, care, and attention as we grow older, we also vow to care for our little family of pets, as they too make their journey through this life with us.

14

Newman

Kristin Kornoelje

Shortly after graduating from college, I announced over dinner at a family gathering that I was looking to get a cat. I'd never had pets growing up, besides a hamster that I had spent years begging for, because my mom was not an animal lover. Now that I was on my own, getting a pet was my top priority, and a cat seemed like a good choice.

No sooner had the words "I'm going to get a cat" come out of my mouth than my cousin Jamie piped up, "I have a cat you can have!"

His name was Newman, and he was a stray that she had found outside her office building. He'd been in a fight with another animal or perhaps had been in an accident of some sort, and he was pretty beat up. Jamie brought him to her vet for medical attention, but because she lived in an apartment and had two cats already, she couldn't take him home with her. So he resided at her office—for a year—until her boss finally told her, "Jamie, I love him, but Newman can't stay here forever. You need to find him a home."

So the timing of my announcement at the dinner table couldn't have been better. Jamie cornered me and gushed about how wonderful Newman was and how excited she was that I was interested, and before I knew it we had arranged for me to meet him. To be honest, I felt ambushed. I mean, it was all happening so fast!

Newman didn't make a great first impression. I don't know what I was imagining, but it wasn't a black cat with a head that looked way too small for his overstuffed sausage of a body. But by this time, I felt obligated to take him; my cousin was thrilled, and besides, it seemed like the right thing to do.

I could go on and on about how taking him home was the best decision I ever made. How his homely little face became the cutest thing in the world to me. That my life wouldn't have been the same without him, and that sometimes the best part of my day was him waiting to greet me at the back door. And all those things would be true. But really, this is a story about Newman and my mom.

Yep, the aforementioned woman who doesn't like animals. Cats in particular. It wasn't that she disliked cats; she loathed them. To her, they were just overgrown rodents.

Mom wasn't on board with the idea of me getting a cat, but she didn't have a whole lot of say in the matter. If she ever found herself over at the house I shared with a roommate, she tolerated Newman's presence fairly well, which was about all I could hope for.

Their relationship started to change about three years after I got him. I decided I wanted to get my own place and moved into a beautiful little apartment in the downtown area. I was excited to have my own space to decorate but had limited funds with which to do so. Around that time, someone gave me a very nice couch with a truly hideous pattern, and my mom volunteered to re-cover it for me. So for about a week, my mom spent the days working on the couch while I was at work.

Just her and Newman.

I was curious how this would go. My super friendly, never-met-a-stranger-he-didn't-love cat and my feline-loathing mother? Here's when I should tell you just how much Newman loved to be around people. He would be waiting at the door for me when I came home literally every day. He would let my friend's toddler pick him up and carry him around without complaint. When I had a roommate, he would take turns sitting on her lap and then mine, back and forth and on and on. And when I had a family gathering at my house, with fifteen of us sitting around in a circle in my living room, he plopped himself right in the middle of the floor. So yeah, this guy loved people.

And my mom's top complaint against cats? "They just seem to know when you don't like them, and they come by you and rub against your legs and want to sit on your lap." It's true, cats have an uncanny way of doing this. And Newman was the friendliest cat I knew.

Imagine my surprise when, at the end of every workday that week, I'd call my mom to see how it went, and she would respond, "Fine." By some miracle, Newman seemed to understand my mom's boundaries. He would watch her progress on the couch and would occasionally come within a foot of her, but at no time did he rub against her leg or try to sit on her lap. What resulted from that week was a begrudging respect and the general opinion that Newman was "all right."

Some time later, I was making plans for a two-week vacation with some friends. Typically when I was away, my dad would look after Newman, stopping over to feed him and clean out the box and play with him for a while. But I was going to be leaving him for longer than I ever had before, and I was feeling guilty. While I was over at my parents' house one Sunday afternoon, I was talking about how I felt bad leaving him and jokingly said, "Maybe he could stay here while I'm gone." To which my mom replied, "I think that would be okay."

I don't think I've ever been so shocked in my life.

So Newman went to live with my parents for two weeks. We established "the Newman zone," which consisted of access to the kitchen, the finished basement, and the family room, where my dad spent the evenings watching TV and reading the paper. My dad loved having him there and was sad to see him go; he especially loved how Newman would be "stealth" (in other words, moving slowly) while sitting in the middle of the paper my dad was trying to read. It's like Newman thought if he moved slowly enough, maybe Dad wouldn't notice a large black cat encroaching on his newspaper.

August 22 Is Take Your Cat to the Vet Day!

It's easy to argue that cats rule the internet and social media. The prevalence of cat memes and feline Instagram stars attest to that. But when it comes to veterinary visits, dogs win, paws down. According to a study by Bayer Animal Health,[1] half of all American pet cats do not see a veterinarian regularly. And Banfield reports that in their more than nine hundred veterinary hospitals, only one cat is seen by a veterinarian for every five dogs.[2] This, despite many studies reporting that there are nearly eight million more pet cats than dogs in the US.

—Susan C. Willett

1. Bayer Veterinary Care Usage Study III: Feline Findings. http://www.bayerdvm.com/show.
2. Banfield State of Pet Health Report, 2016.http://www.banfield.com/.

But what about Mom? I asked her how it went, and she said she survived but was glad to be rid of him. My dad disputed this, though. "Waaaait a minute," he said with a twinkle in his eye. Then he turned to me. "You should've heard the way she talked to him, in this high-pitched voice like he was a baby. She loved having him here."

From that point on, my mom and Newman were buds. There were no pets or cuddles, but there was a nice friendship. I bought a house that needed a lot of work, and my parents, who were do-it-yourselfers, basically redid the place (I know, I'm lucky!). My mom spent many a day completing home-improvement projects with Newman for company. She always talked to him in that baby voice and would frequently fill me in on what he got up to while I was gone. One time, she took off the grate in the floor that led to the ducts of my house and then forgot to put the grate back. Some time later, she noticed she hadn't seen Newman in a while, and realized with a sinking feeling that he was exploring the ducts of my house. As she told me the story, I could just picture it. My mom crouched on the floor, calling down through the ducts, trying to keep the panic from her voice as she coaxed him back. Newman would periodically meow back until he finally decided to come out. She was relieved she wouldn't have to tell me that she had killed my cat. (I still chuckle when I think of how often after that day Newman would sit by that grate and stare at it and occasionally whine and meow, as if wanting to relive the wonderful adventure he'd had.)

Every time my mom came over, the first thing that would come out of her mouth was "Where's Newman?" And as soon as she saw him, she'd say in that high-pitched voice, "Hi, Newman! Whatcha doin', Newman?" (I probably heard those words a hundred times.) And in all those years, Newman never so much as rubbed against her leg or tried to climb on her lap. Now that truly was a miracle!

Newman was about two when I got him from my cousin Jamie, and I had him with me for thirteen years. During his last year, he got sick, and the vet told me that he would have good days and bad days until the bad days outnumbered the good, and that would be his time. He had a lot of good days until one very bad day when he declined quickly. It was over the weekend, and I was panicked because my vet's office was closed, and I knew I couldn't let him suffer until Monday. I called my mom sobbing because I knew I had to find an emergency vet and was too emotional to make phone calls. So she made calls for me and picked me up and went with me to the emergency vet. She was with me in the room to say good-bye. I'll never forget how she told him she loved him and cried for him just as much as I did.

I've thought many times over the years how amazing it was that my offhand comment at a family gathering led to thirteen years with my little dude. I can't help but think that it was meant to be. And not just for me, but for my mom too.

I wish I could tell you that she loves cats now. She doesn't. But she is able to tolerate them much more than she used to. More than anything, Newman helped her understand the love that exists between a person and their pet and the joy and laughter an animal (yes, even a cat!) can bring to your life.

My life was better for having Newman in it. I think my mom's was too.

15

The Trouble with Harry

Melody Carlson

I've almost always had cats. When I was a child, we had numerous and various feline family members—from alley cats to a big gorgeous seal-point Siamese who lived well into her twenties. As an adult with my own family, I had more cats. But then we moved into the mountains, right next to the National Forest, and I was warned that cats and small dogs were also known as "coyote food" if you let them outside. Not only did we have coyotes slipping right through our yard, we experienced the occasional cougar as well.

Even so, I decided to have a house cat that I was determined to confine to the great indoors. I adopted a sweet tiger-striped cat named Bob and kept him housebound throughout the long, cold winter. But when springtime came, Bob seemed to pine away, longingly looking out our sunroom windows . . . and one fine summer day, my husband defended Bob's right to go outside. I still remember seeing him sunning his pretty striped coat on a big boulder outside our sunroom windows. Bob disappeared that same day, and we never saw him again.

So, I decided, no more cats.

But a few years later, a strange-looking cat showed up on our deck in midwinter. This cat was quite large with an extra-long tail, and sort of resembled a raccoon. And he looked like trouble. With his dark and matted hair and an ear that had been nipped by something, he had a wild, almost scary, look to him. Whenever we stepped out onto our large covered porch, he would take off like a shot, seeking refuge beneath our deck. We assumed he was a feral cat and probably wouldn't last long with coyotes and cougars about. Not to mention the occasional skunks that snuck around. Or the pesky raccoons that frequently raided my fish pond.

And yet, this cat stuck around. Although he looked like trouble—and I worried he too might raid my fish pond—I began to feel sorry for the poor animal. It was winter and icy cold . . . so I decided to put out some cat food and water. I honestly didn't expect this obviously homeless cat to be around for long. Between the harsh weather and the nearby predators, the odds were stacked against him.

But this wild-looking cat continued to make his appearances and he continued to eat the food. We jokingly named him Harry because of his shaggy coat. But he was still mysteriously evasive. And we continued to assume he was a feral cat.

After a few weeks, I became concerned. What if this cat was dangerous? Or unhealthy? What if he passed some disease on to our dog? So I called our vet for advice, and she confirmed the cat could have rabies. She offered us a "live cat trap," advising us to bring him in as soon as possible.

That was when my husband stepped in. Now, Chris is not a cat person. His first reaction to cats is to keep a cool distance. And he's almost always opposed to having a cat for a pet. But for some reason, he decided to make an attempt at befriending Harry. So he positioned himself on the deck with some cat food and called out to the cat. Watching from inside, I felt pretty skeptical—not to mention worried. What if Harry had rabies or infected claws or ticks or whatever?

But Chris was patient, talking quietly and waiting. And to our utter amazement, Harry walked right up to him. He even let Chris pet him. And, according to Chris, he actually purred. Then Chris casually picked him up, put him in his pickup, and drove him to the vet. Just like that. No big deal.

Come to find out, Harry was a Maine coon cat with an electronic ID chip that was registered with the vet. He belonged to someone in our neighborhood, and his real name was Alexander (which we didn't think fit him). According to the vet, Alexander had inhabited a house with *six* other cats! And according to the vet, Alexander did not like other cats. Not at all. He would either avoid them or pick fights. The vet called Alexander's owners, and they said that since Alexander had adopted us, we could adopt him. So my husband agreed to this, and we became the owners of a big Maine coon cat that we called Harry.

But wait a minute, that's not exactly true. I think Harry became the owner of us. The trouble with Harry was that nobody could own a tough character like him. He was an independent outdoor cat with a mind of his own. He had no interest in living indoors or being coddled. Even the way he walked seemed to suggest he didn't need anybody. Maybe that's why my husband liked him so much. Harry was no namby-pamby.

And yet, if we were sitting outside, Harry would gladly hop onto our laps—when he felt like it. He would happily sit there, purring and allowing us to pet him or groom his coat. But at other times he just wanted his space to be left to his own. And we let him. I think he'd been attracted to our property because of the covered porches and expansive decks, providing him secure spaces to take refuge. So we decided to let him do as he pleased. I made him a nice warm bed, which he sometimes used, but often did not.

The longer we shared our home with Harry, the more we grew to love and admire him. He was a great mouser, and he even became friends with our yellow Lab Audrey. Although he preferred being outside, he would visit my writing studio if I left the door open on a sunny day. He would lie down right next to Audrey, perfectly content. And once we started to appreciate the classic characteristics of a Maine coon cat, we realized how truly beautiful he was. He had a handsome large head and wide jade-green eyes, a multi-layered coat that allowed him to be comfortable in all weather, oversized fuzzy paws, an extra-long tail, and a laid-back intelligent personality that endeared him to us.

One of our favorite Harry memories happened one evening. We spied him outside one of our floor-to-ceiling windows. Just complacently sitting on the deck, right next to his food bowl, looking directly into the house. But on the other side of his bowl sat a large skunk! Both of them stared into the house, and neither of them made a move. Harry appeared completely composed—almost as if he was calmly warning the skunk to stay away from his food bowl. We watched in silent amazement, knowing better than to lift a finger because Harry obviously had the situation under control. Eventually the skunk moved on—without making a stink.

We enjoyed many years with our sweet Harry. He reminded us that, despite living on the edge of the wilderness, we didn't have to give up on having a cat. We'd just needed the right kind of cat. And Harry needed the right kind of home. We were happy to give it to him.

16

Thirty-Six Piccolos

Kathleen J. McClatchey

I grabbed my piccolo and purse and raced toward the front door. I was late, as usual. I had recently read that optimists are generally late, because they think they can get an unrealistic number of tasks completed before they leave the house. In my case, I wasn't sure it was so much optimism that made me late as it was my penchant for adding critters to our family, a growing challenge for my only-child, never-had-a-pet husband. When I once pointed out to him that he knew I was an animal lover when he proposed to me, he noted that when he married me, I had one cat and one dog, and now, in addition to our three kids, we were up to thirty-five nonhuman family members.

Our son Benjamin, often described euphemistically by his elementary schoolteachers as "creative" or "marching to the sound of his own drum," at one time went through a stage where he embellished descriptions of our family. We had some good laughs with his teachers when we assured them that we had not sent him off by himself (at eight years of age!) on a charter ship to go deep-sea fishing for marlin, nor was his father a former Manchester United soccer player. One teacher then informed us that the really crazy thing Benjamin had told them was that he lived in a zoo with over thirty pets. I had the distinct impression that the school staff never looked at us quite the same after we confessed that we did indeed have an extensive menagerie. In my defense, many of them were birds, fish, or reptiles, confined to their habitats, so at least half of the thirty weren't roaming the house.

We loved all of our animals dearly, but they did increase the leaving-home checklist, as well as create an obstacle course to be carefully navigated, one that was presently seriously slowing my urgent progress toward the front door. The August heat had driven the two Saint Bernards and the Standard Poodle inside to lounge in the air-conditioning. They were all happily sprawled out asleep, each taking up most of the floor space in the rooms on my direct path to get out of the house. In addition, three of our five cats, alert to behaviors that signaled my departure, leaped into action to make sure they had adequate food before I left. After all, who knew how long I might be gone? I wouldn't want them to starve in my absence, would I?

I finally made it out the door and into my car. I glanced at the dashboard clock, calculating how much time I had to make it in and out of the drugstore without being too late to rehearsal. Promptness was important, given that I was responsible for leading said rehearsal. I was coaching the piccolo section in my daughter's marching band. It was a fun throwback to my flute-teaching days as well as a great chance to do something with my teenage daughter. Julianna's high school was holding their weeklong band camp at a college about an hour away.

The high school music program was amazing, with a marching band of close to three hundred students. When the band director asked me to help out, I eagerly accepted. At the last minute, I thought to ask him how many piccolo players there were in the section. It was a good thing he was on his way out of the room, as he answered over his shoulder that there were "thirty-five or thirty-six."

Thirty-six piccolo players? My head throbbed at the thought of it.

Those of you unfamiliar with the piccolo may not understand my reaction. The piccolo is a tiny flute that plays high notes. *Very* high notes. Very high notes can be extremely difficult to play and get exactly right. A close approximation, yes, but exactly the right pitch—it's something of a long shot dependent on the skill of the piccolo player. There is a reason why symphony orchestras rarely have more than one piccolo player. One piccolo player playing a little off-key isn't usually much of a problem, since no one else is playing that same super-high note. It might be a wee bit (or a country mile) north or south of the desired pitch. Generally more than half the audience can't really hear all the notes the piccolo is playing anyway; age-related hearing loss starts with needing to hear the high notes louder in order to hear them at all. One piccolo player can generate only so much sound, so many of the concertgoers never even hear the performer's imperfections.

However, thirty-six piccolo players playing all at once, in a rehearsal in an enclosed space? That many piccolos playing thirty-six different variations of one note competing for attention cannot be ignored. Even Beethoven on his path to deafness would have likely left the room in pain.

I hurtled my car into a parking place at the drugstore and raced inside. I had once noted with interest that this drugstore sold large jars of foam earplugs. I had no idea why any one individual would want a hundred of the things, but for me today the large quantity was fortuitous and essential. I sped to the register, clutching one of the jars.

Back in my car, I hurried down the road, pleased that my stop had taken less time than anticipated. I drove making sure I was not going any faster than five miles over the posted fifty-five-miles-per-hour speed limit. I felt that the potential of thirty-six high school piccolo players playing without supervision (increasing the possibility of creating thirty-six new hearing impairments) justified my transgression.

At that moment ahead of me, I saw a strange object on the double yellow line in the middle of the road. I slowed down slightly, trying to make out what it was. From a distance it looked like a small orange fuzzy child's blanket in a heap. I slowed down a little more, when suddenly the heap moved slightly, and two enormous green eyes looked straight at me. I slammed on the brakes and skidded to a stop on the side of the road. I looked back at the orange mound and realized in astonishment that it was an orange kitten—an exceedingly bedraggled and forlorn-looking tiny kitten.

I grew up with a father who had much in common with Dr. Doolittle, the veterinarian who could talk to animals. We had a never-ending stream of critters in our home, all of whom loved the rest of us but worshiped my father. Dad was not a veterinarian, but he certainly cared greatly for the animals with whom we share this world. Dad would always say, "We can't take care of every animal in the world. But if an animal comes across our path, then there is no question—we are responsible to care for that animal, forever."

My mother frequently accused my father of having created some neon sign over our rural home, invisible to humans but highly visible to any two- or four-footed nonhuman creature, that said "Animals needing a home, come here!" She felt it was the only reasonable explanation for why a steady stream of strays seemed to turn up on our doorstep, at a rate far beyond what could possibly be normal. Certainly, we didn't know anyone else who seemed to be as well prepared for another Noah's ark. I didn't mind, since I shared Dad's love of all the additions.

Hearing my dad's admonition in my mind, I was out of the car in a flash. I crept toward the kitten, watching for cars. I was afraid the creature would run into the tall grass at the side of the road at the sight of me, but the poor creature just looked up at me with enormous swollen eyes. He was a mess. His eyes were so horribly infected and draining that he had no fur at all on his face. I could literally see the fleas hopping on him, he was desperately skinny, and his orange fur was a matted, bedraggled mess.

But what really tore at my heart was his mood. He seemed totally defeated and depressed. It occurred to me that perhaps he had positioned himself in the middle of this road in the hopes that one of the vehicles racing by would end his misery. I gently picked him up. A tick dropped onto my arm. I flicked it off and held the kitten by the loose skin on the back of his neck. He hung limply, those enormous eyes fixed on me.

I climbed back in the car and held him with one hand over the passenger seat, while with the other hand I turned the car around and headed back to town. Within minutes, I was in our vet's clinic, still holding the kitten at arm's length. Everyone at the clinic knew me well, given the number of critters we brought in and out. (After one particularly expensive visit, my long-suffering husband asked if maybe the clinic took paycheck direct deposit?) I handed the kitten across the high counter to the only mildly surprised vet tech, who grabbed a towel and wrapped up the pitiable kitten, gently cuddling the skinny orange lump. I told him to have the vet do what he could for the little thing, and I would stop by on my way home to settle the bill.

When I arrived at rehearsal, the piccolo players had thankfully not played enough to permanently impair their hearing. I sternly admonished them that no one was to play another note in an enclosed space until we were all well-armed with earplugs, which they found highly entertaining. I explained my tardiness by letting them know about the kitten, which resulted in an extended time of cooing and motherly expressions of concern (only three of the thirty-six students were guys).

Two weeks later we were finally able to bring the kitten home from the vet. The clinic staff named the kitten Elliott, and his transformation was astounding. He eventually grew into a very impressive twenty-pound cat with a thick, luxurious, brilliantly orange coat. The most impressive transformation was in his approach to the world. Gone was the beaten-down animal I had picked up off the asphalt. In his place was a cat who was buoyant, full of affection and personality, eager to play and interact with everything and everyone. If anyone in the house sat down, Elliott immediately appeared to curl up in their lap, purring enthusiastically. He even purred in his sleep.

We had friends, a young couple, who fell in love with Elliott as soon as we brought him home from the vet (even though his face, though no longer inflamed, only had a hint of fur on it). They asked if they could have him, and given our large menagerie, I was only too happy to have him go to a new home. We agreed that if they ever couldn't take care of him, they would return him to us.

Elliott happily settled in his new home and family. They doted on him and thoroughly delighted in seeing his personality and beauty emerge as he grew. However, over the year the man's previous mild cat allergy gradually increased in severity. Eventually even walking into their apartment caused his eyes to swell and his unending sneezes to start. Elliott needed to come back to us.

I admit I was delighted that we had Elliott once again. He quickly bonded to another of our cats, Jacque, a tuxedo junkyard rescue, and they happily raced around the house together, engaging in various shenanigans, including never-ending games of tag. They especially relished competitions to see who could fit their ample bodies into the smallest box or other intriguing spaces.

We did face one slight challenge as a result of the months Elliott spent in his other home. The man's work schedule required that he get up every morning at 4:30 a.m. This fact was clearly indelibly inscribed in Elliott's brain as "all male humans are to get up at 4:30 a.m." Anyone who has had to deal with a cat determined to wake one up knows that it is almost useless to resist. The gentle rubs, loud purrs, and gentle paw on the cheek will usually, after some time, turn into more resolute tactics: the claw slowly extended to prick a chin or a bite (just short of breaking the skin) on a vulnerable earlobe.

While we had heard of Elliott's morning ritual, it hadn't occurred to us that this might be something we would have to deal with in a household with three males (my husband and two sons). Our sons quickly learned to close their bedroom doors at night to avoid Elliott's 4:30 a.m. insistence that they get up *now*. My daughter and I were totally exempt from Elliott's attention—he didn't care if we slept in till noon. My husband was not so fortunate. Keeping our bedroom door closed all night was not an option. One of our Saint Bernards checked in on each of the kids at least three times a night, returning to settle in on the floor at the end of our bed, her established nighttime sleeping spot. Getting up six times a night to let Molly in and out of our room was also not conducive to a reasonable night's sleep.

Reluctantly we finally took to closing Elliott in the basement at night, with his cat buddy Jacque for company. When I opened the basement door in the morning, they would both shoot out and then entertain me with reenactments of their nighttime chases. As soon as I poured my coffee and sat down for my morning quiet time, Elliott would lithely jump onto my lap, curl up happily, and together we would prepare ourselves for the day ahead. There is nothing quite like a warm soft purring cat in my lap to remind me of the important things in life and the special joy of getting to share our lives with other loves, including furry four-footed ones.

I spend a lot of time speeding through life, five miles or more over the speed limit, hurrying to get to a destination that may not actually be the most important one for that day. Every once in a while I remember with gratitude that day when I was mindful enough to notice a small heap of orange fur in the middle of the road. That day I pulled off to the side and did something important. When those sad green eyes met mine, it was a gift. I picked up an unwanted, flea-bitten kitten out of the road and was gifted a fun-loving, purring, daily reminder of the joy of living in concert with God's creation and creatures.

Elliott was kind of a classy name for such a scruffy kitten, but we liked it. I thought for a time that we should name him Piccolo, given that if it weren't for those thirty-six high school students with their potentially ear-piercing piccolos, I never would have been driving down that road on that day right at the time a sad kitten positioned himself in such a dangerous place. Such is the serendipity of life. Only much later did I learn that the name Elliott comes from the Hebrew name "Elijah." In the Old Testament of the Bible, Elijah was a prophet and a miracle worker who spent his life turning people's attention from things that might look important but were not, to focusing on what is real and essential to living a meaningful life.

108

It was, indeed, the perfect name for Elliott, a scrawny kitten plucked from the tarmac who grew into our remarkable orange cat. Elliott, true to his name, never missed a chance to remind us that sometimes the most important thing in the world is to make room in our lives for one of God's creations—to sit and be a settling place for warm cuddles, soft purrs, a quiet time, and love.

17

When Wild Calls

DJ Perry

Cats are a mystery in their behavior and actions. They must have days when they wake up and feel like, *Today I will not wear the cloak of domestication*. Perhaps the surge in TV and nature shows left playing on televisions to entertain our pets has somehow sparked the wild within them. Across the landscapes of Africa and India the lords and ladies of Cat-Kind rule. They can be seen on the screen exploring, stalking, hunting, and just being wild and free. I've seen our cats watch the TV in wonder as if some primitive gene was being tickled and awakened.

The lady-cat of our house, Lulu, was very different from her two ragamuffin brothers. Jamieson, once shy, was now the social cat that all other cats in the neighborhood enjoyed being around. Conversely, Demetri thought the world was his and was always ready to prove it. Unlike the almost always matted fur of her brothers, Lulu's grooming was purrfection. Sleek, glossy, and black, grace in every step. Her interest did not usually go beyond the human castle that she claimed as her domain. The brothers would often go on adventures, sometimes even overnight. Worry would give way to relief when the two boys stumbled home after a few nights gone. What adventures they had we'll never know. Obvious hunger and a few scratches painted a picture of carousing and possible conflict on their journey. Lulu gave little mind to such things when waking from a nap in one of her many pampered places.

Our property backs up to a park and provides a great opportunity for adventure. We occasionally worried because of the random off-leash dog or the giant bird of prey that scooped up smaller animals in the area. Cars are always a concern, but the cats seemed to be good at avoiding that danger. Many cats lived in our neighborhood. Some were strays and others adventurers like our own, shrugging off their human servants for a bit of excitement. On any given night, the back and forth threatening meows of two dominant toms could be heard. Most ended peacefully and others after a whirl of claws and fur. I think our Demetri got himself caught up in this kitty fight club on occasion. He would come home hungry and with a few new patches of fur missing.

Lulu had been fixed long ago, but one day something seemed to be making her restless. She took quick walks out the doggie door to pace the patio porch and gaze off toward the park. I was unsure what could get the queen out of her comfort zone and out into the wild. She was even caught leaving the safety of the deck and wandering around bushes, trees, and high grass. These explorations again were completely out of character for her. Something was going on inside her little kitty brain, and we were unsure just what that might be. Some believe cats wander off before they die, but Lulu was not in any kind of health distress.

The days that followed included small excursions where she would be gone for a few hours at a time. She would appear and disappear as she desired, like a Japanese ninja. Her mission was top secret, and she would reveal nothing about her comings and goings.

One night as the streetlights came on and night fell, Lulu was nowhere to be found. Her normal haunts were empty. No wide-eyed Lulu peering from the top of the stairs or from beneath one of her favorite hidey-holes. Where could she be?

Lulu could disappear in the house for what seemed like days, but she was just avoiding people and doing her solo thing. But after years of coexisting, you start to know all your cat's hiding places. An extensive search led us to the conclusion that Lulu was *not* in the house. No letter, no phone call, she just up and left. If Lulu had any financial value, we might have thought she had been catnapped. But could these few weeks of strange behavior and meandering into the wild have led to a full-on case of running away from home? Did she go on vacation? UFO abduction?

A few days went by with no Lulu.

She and one of her brothers, Demetri the troublemaker, did not see eye to eye. Her hissing and swipes at the bothersome "Gray Rat" were commonplace in our home. Maybe she had enough of living with him and his constant taunts. While both brothers had her in weight, she was capable of being no-nonsense when she had to be. Our ninety-plus-pound pit bull discovered how feisty she could be if pushed. So we knew, save the improbable unseen car, she was quite capable of protecting herself.

After a week we became quite concerned. Our only thread of hope was that on a few occasions I could have sworn that I heard her meow from the park. Was she being kept by someone else? Maybe willingly because she wasn't having to deal with her brother and his teasing? I decided I would have to have my own little adventure. A rescue adventure.

Walking the park, I came to a section of woods behind an abandoned house. I could see a large oak tree had fallen, revealing

113

a massive root system. The part aboveground was fanned outward, looking like the head of Medusa, full of sticky snakes. I had to take a second glance as I got closer because I noticed a cat stretched out on a root limb. Was it Lulu? No. But I saw another, and another, and another. There were no fewer than twenty cats all lying on these exposed roots. It felt like something right out of a Stephen King book. As I got closer, the cats scattered, disappearing into the overgrown grass. But I did catch a glimpse of a sleek black cat—Lulu.

What was going on here? Had she joined a cult? Had she been kidnapped by a gang of cats? Or was this a meeting to decide the time had come for cats to rise up and take over the world? It was the craziest thing to witness, and it reminded me of all those lionesses lounging on the tree branches in Africa, beating the heat.

I yelled for Lulu to get home. We assume cats understand what we are saying, and they just might. I returned home and decided to just wait. Sure enough, that night the plastic flap on the dog door caught our attention, and Lulu strutted inside. A drink of water. A bite of food. She went to curl in one of her spots.

After that day, Lulu never ventured forth like that again. She did not even wander the yard beyond the occasional walk on the deck before returning inside. Maybe she'd wanted one big adventure in her lifetime, I don't know. I can't say for sure that she needed rescuing, but it was one of the craziest things to behold.

I do catch her watching those nature programs from time to time—the ones that feature her larger wild relatives surviving in the outdoors. I think she has gotten that wanderlust out of her system and is content watching it on the television. But you never know when that adventure bug may strike again. I sometimes wonder how many cats have joined that mob of felines by the abandoned house. I counted around twenty-two that day.

Watch out. The cats might be planning something.

18

Spirit and the Miracle 4

Kathrine Diedre Smith

I am no stranger to rescue, but this one was different. A woman who had trapped a feral momma kitty the previous day to be spayed called me. She said that she had been trying to trap the feral cat for weeks and knew she was pregnant. When she did capture the cat, she noticed that the cat appeared to no longer have a big belly. Her veterinarian told her after the cat's surgery that the momma cat had given birth six to eight weeks earlier, and that the kittens were weaned, off on their own, and most likely frolicking in a field somewhere. The woman told me that about a week earlier the feral cat looked as big around as a basketball. For some reason she chose to believe the vet rather than her own observations, so she never looked for any kittens.

I asked the woman for the location of where she had trapped the feral momma. If the cat was recently pregnant, there were babies somewhere in trouble. A strong cold front with heavy rains had just come through, leaving our area with unseasonably chilly, windy conditions and drenched with standing water. We were facing record-low temperatures that night for this part of Texas, with below freezing temperatures. It had been over thirty hours since the woman trapped the momma cat. Her babies, if they were still alive, had not received any nourishment, warmth, or stimulation (newborn kittens cannot eliminate on their own), and the thought of any kittens suffering this way was too much for me to sit back and do nothing. I had to try to find them. Time was of the essence.

The woman had trapped the momma cat at a construction site with an expansive area of large open fields, nearby businesses, and two very busy intersections on either side. A new fitness facility was being built in this section of an already growing development area, and there was a temporary construction building on site.

Realizing my own very real physical limitations as a human being in search of young kittens in quite an expansive area, I knew I needed additional support. So I reached out to my own cat, a blind rescue kitty who had found me almost two years earlier. His name is Spirit, and he is extraordinary. Someone cruel had permanently blinded him when he was just a kitten, but somehow he escaped and navigated through busy streets and neighborhoods and found a way to gain entry inside my brick-enclosed courtyard—through a closed iron gate. I woke up early one morning to find him literally on my doorstep, waiting for me. This classic mackerel tabby and I formed a powerful connection, which quickly became a bond greater than any one of us ever expected. I had worked extensively with Spirit and harness- and leash-trained him, and we shared many adventures together.

Not knowing what we might encounter, I put Spirit's harness and lead on, loaded him up, and away we drove to the area where the feral momma cat had been trapped. I parked beside the large temporary construction site trailer and went inside to introduce

116

myself to the workers and to let them know we were there to search for the kittens. The people were very cordial but clearly skeptical. They told me that they knew there was a feral cat that appeared to be pregnant earlier, and one of their workers had been feeding her behind the temporary building before she was trapped. I asked if I could search the area, and they said go for it—I could search anywhere I wanted to, though no one expected me to find anything.

I walked around the portable building, which was fully skirted along the bottom with the exception of an area close to the back corner. Mounds of dirt, high weeds, and thick mud were only a part of what I encountered. What caught my attention was the large floating septic system where water and human waste from inside the portable building overflowed into the cold squishy mud. Adjacent to the septic system was a small cut-out section, allowing narrow access underneath the portable building.

I looked inside the small opening and saw an extremely low to the ground crawl space. It was cold, dark, muddy, and murky, and I immediately felt overwhelmed. No one else was there except me and my blind cat, and given the low crawl space and unknown conditions underneath, my heart sank. I needed to search underneath the building, which was about the size of a three-bedroom, double-wide trailer. It was even more daunting to see one temporary floor jack holding the rear entrance up. A single layer of cinder blocks had been placed intermittently, along with scrap pieces of wood scattered throughout, to brace the entire weight of the portable building. An array of metal and PVC pipe was attached to the underside of the trailer, which further compromised the already very limited crawl space. Long metal beams mounted beneath the structure allowed only about twelve inches of uneven clearance space to crawl underneath.

The area under the trailer was so daunting that I did not feel safe going into this dark, cold, wet area with only one entry/exit point. But the need to search for the abandoned kittens was more pressing, because time was of the essence. So I said a prayer and called a dear friend who lived close by. I asked her if she would be willing to venture into the unknown with Spirit and me to search for kittens under the construction site trailer. To my surprise, she agreed!

Now, this is no ordinary friend. This woman is incredibly gorgeous and chic—a former cheerleader, homecoming princess . . . the kind of person you would never expect to be willing to crawl underneath a dark, murky trailer with a floating portable septic system. She heard me say "I need your help," and that was all it took—she was in. I described to her the dark, muddy, and murky conditions, gave her the directions to get there, and she gathered up some flashlights, changed her clothes, and drove to the location. It was now over thirty-one hours since the momma cat had been caught and who knew how long since the babies had been without nourishment or support.

When my friend arrived, so did a greater sense of hope. For me. I am extremely claustrophobic. So much so that I feel panicked anytime I'm in a small space, and am prone to panic attacks. Just putting my head in a small, enclosed opening makes me dizzy, so the idea of going completely underneath such a confined crawl space . . . well, I was having difficulty breathing. Still, I couldn't let my friend go underneath that dark trailer alone, and I wouldn't let my blind cat go in without me.

So I took a deep breath and ventured into the unknown. With flashlight in hand, I could see that the area was even worse than what I first saw. About a third of the ground underneath the trailer was underwater, a cesspool of stinky murk. Every time someone flushed the toilet inside the building, we heard it—along with a slow gur-gur-gurgle of overflowing fluid rising up from the cold, thick mud. There was no need to search that side of the area.

Nothing we would want to find could survive in that muck. So we focused on the other side.

We had to keep our heads low and army crawl on our bellies underneath the trailer. We used our elbows and splayed our back legs out to navigate the area. I decided to take Spirit off lead so that he could search areas underneath the trailer where we could not reach. Because of the unevenness of the ground, sometimes the ceiling height was as low as six to eight inches, so there was no way that my friend or I could get to those areas where scrap wood and patches of old dead weeds were. My friend questioned letting Spirit loose, thinking he might panic or make a run out the opening, but I know my Spirit; there is a deeper connection where we listen and trust each other, and he would never leave me.

The challenge was how to guide Spirit to search the specific areas I wanted him to. Since he can't see, he is not able to follow my hand motions. Nor does he know specific words such as *left* or *right* or *straight*. What he does know is my voice, and he is a fast learner by following the vocal cues and praise I give him, as well as having a strong sense of adventure.

So I unclipped his lead and encouraged him to explore. Spirit walked a straight line past me, then paused to take in the new smells. "Keep going, Spirit," I coaxed, and he continued moving forward all the way to the end of the trailer. Once he reached the end, I wanted him to search along the right side, but he turned left. I simply said "Nope," and he changed direction. The moment he moved right, I said, "Good job, keep going"—and he did! It was amazing to see this little blind cat taking his cues from me and following them. He became a remarkable search kitty, and he took his job seriously. He followed my cues, covering areas where my friend and I could not crawl to because it was so low to the ground, but not too low for an adventurous cat, sniffing and searching all along the underside of the trailer. Several times, Spirit turned and ventured toward an area behind me, but I redirected him to come back and search other places that needed to be checked.

After spending around an hour and a half crawling on our bellies in the cold, wet mud underneath the portable building, it seemed we had checked everywhere for the kittens. The situation appeared to be hopeless. The only life we heard were the footsteps above us from the people inside the trailer. Every time we heard the toilet flush, the ground gurgled, and we grimaced. We started to army crawl our way across the mud toward the exit when I noticed something. Spirit kept stopping and pointing his head to an area of subfloor under the trailer. It was the same area he kept going back to when I was redirecting him to move forward. This kitty seemed fixated on this one specific area. It happened to be where the toilet and plumbing from the subfloor came out and connected to the floating septic system. Perhaps Spirit was intrigued by the vibrations from the plumbing.

But then I saw him raise his paw up, as he was standing tall and stiff, and he focused intently on this area of subfloor. He was alerting us. My friend belly crawled over to where Spirit stood and cautiously reached up inside the dark subfloor, removing thick layers of itchy fiberglass insulation. Then I heard her gasp—there was a tiny kitten! With eyes barely open and itty-bitty ears folded forward, the silver tiger-striped kitten was alive! My friend removed another large chunk of insulation, and there in the back of the subfloor were three more kittens, making a total of four—two silver tabbies and two solid black babies—and they were all alive! What a miracle!

My friend gently handed each kitten down to me, and I placed them on a towel. They were so tiny and fragile, maybe ten days old. It had been more than thirty-three hours since their feral momma had been trapped, and who knows how long since they last nursed. The evening was quickly approaching, and I wanted to get these kittens stabilized. Their mother was recuperating from her surgery somewhere else, but fortunately, I was fostering two rescued momma cats at my house at the time, and one had kittens who were approximately the same age as these four.

Once I got the kittens home, I looked them over carefully, checking for any fleas or injuries, and discovered they were all girls. I called them the Miracle 4 Girls, and began introducing them to the newest momma foster cat named CC (Country Cat). The kittens began screaming and squirming as soon as I placed them with the young momma cat. They were starving and their little bodies were toxic from not being fed or stimulated for over a day and a half. Although I am an experienced bottle baby feeder, I was greatly concerned about them and their extremely delicate state. I felt that their best chance of survival was through the constant nurture and nutrition that only a momma cat can provide. But CC couldn't handle the stress of their distress.

I reached out to the other momma cat I was fostering, named Juno. She was much older, more calm and experienced than the other foster momma. However, her kittens were about four weeks old and at least three times larger than the ones we just rescued. Also, Juno was not as prolific with her milk production as the younger mom. But she was extremely patient and nurturing, and Juno had formed a strong bond with me.

So I created a soft nest for the rescued kittens, separate from Juno's babies, and introduced the older rescue momma cat to the orphan girls. They started crying again, desperate and starving but unable to nurse. This time, the more experienced Juno stepped up and began gently washing and stimulating each one of the orphan kittens, methodically tending to each little baby. She stayed up all night long with the kittens, comforting them, slowly and patiently nursing them back to health, removing the accumulated toxins in their tiny bodies, and providing essential nourishment to their delicate systems. I stayed up all night with her and them as well, supporting this remarkable momma cat and making sure her own kittens were happy while their mother devoted herself to the Miracle 4 Girls. I fully believe that Juno was responsible for saving their lives that night.

After a full twenty-four hours of stabilizing the Miracle 4 Girls with Juno, who only left the new kittens long enough to quickly eat, drink, and nurse her own kittens, I tried reintroducing the Miracle 4 Girls to CC, the younger momma cat. This time, CC accepted them. The kittens were much calmer now, in a better place, thanks to Juno. Each of the foster momma cats in my home had five kittens of her own, so in order to help support all fourteen kittens, I thought it would be best to rotate the Miracle 4 Girls throughout the day and night between the two nursing momma cats. A feat I had never tried before, this remarkable maternal arrangement worked great—and was phenomenal! The tiny Miracle 4 Girls were no longer orphans; they now had two loving, nurturing moms.

These momma cats were not related, and they did not like each other at all, but they shared a deep love and affection for these precious kittens! Each time I rotated the girls to a different momma, their adopted mother immediately took over the care and nourishment for them. The kittens shared the best of both worlds, grew stronger every day, and gained exceptional social skills. Because CC's babies were close in age to the Miracle 4 Girls, I was able to successfully introduce them to her family after about two weeks, and they gained a remarkably rich relationship with their new siblings. No one ever suffered any kind of setback or illness whatsoever, and I had two amazing momma cats to thank for that.

The Miracle 4 Girls grew up to become incredibly friendly, socialized, and highly adaptable to new situations. When they were old enough and completely vetted, the sisters were adopted together in pairs to two loving homes. One pair now lives in Michigan, while the other two girls live in Illinois.

I am most grateful for my friend Marilyn, who heeded my call and was willing to venture into a cold, dark place, army crawl underneath a portable construction trailer in mud and who knows what else, all for the sake of rescue. Special thanks to Juno and CC, two remarkable formerly homeless momma cats, who really stepped up and helped save and nurture the precious Miracle 4 Girls, who had been abandoned and left starving and unstimulated for more than thirty-four hours.

And to my amazing Spirit, the little blind cat who survived horrific abuse as a kitten and somehow found me. His courage, devotion, intelligence, and tenacity give me strength and hope every single day. I could not have done this without him. I could not have achieved any of this search and rescue success without the cooperative support of my dear friend and these phenomenal felines. We can achieve great things through faith and the right support.

19

Finding Home

Kristin M. Avery

K at stood at the front of the carrier, smelling steamy August for the first time in three years. The drive from the shelter to our house was only ten minutes but seemed longer, more stretched out that day. Street scenes passed through her eyes like 70-millimeter film. Cars, bikes, delivery trucks, children and dogs playing, mothers with strollers, old men on stoops and park benches. The world was still here, and so was she. Kat didn't know where she was going, only that she was going with me. I was her home; she knew it before I knew it, but we both knew it then.

Kat was one of the first cats admitted to the shelter. We weren't even officially open yet. Donated supplies in boxes, stacks of blankets and beds, metal cages still flat and folded up. The whole place freshly painted and kind of dreamlike except for the intake calls. Kat was the result of one of those early, frantic, please-take-my-cat-now calls.

Her name was originally Katrina, but I shortened it to Kat. Like many shelter cats, she had bounced around between homes in her ten years. Most recently, she was part of a domestic dispute that left her locked in a basement, a furless spot on her nose from trying to escape. The woman on the phone begged us to take Kat. Her husband was threatening to hurt her—and something about the way Kat was crying in the background made me suspect that he already had. I couldn't say no.

I remember peering into her cage that first night. Her fur was midnight black aside from a few white strands on her neck. She glared at me, through me, defiantly, to prove she wasn't afraid. But I didn't believe her and she knew it and that's probably where our life together began.

Looking back, I think Kat pegged me pretty early on as her only ticket out of the shelter. After graduating from her cage to the office area, she followed me around with a kind of guttural growl. She sometimes hopped up on the desk next to me, close but not too close, almost daring me to pet her. But I knew she was testing me so I didn't yet try.

Kat didn't care much for other cats and she was choosy with humans too. She was tiny, the size of an almost adolescent kitten, but as fierce as a New York City opera lady with a cane. Adopters skipped right over her; no one was looking for an older, sassy black cat. Kat had been hurt and it showed, as she swatted and hissed at even the kindest volunteers. She had a sharp-tongued, angry meow that, combined with her mean right hook, scared people and cats away.

I don't remember when things changed. But Kat started waiting for me in the front window, day and night, January or July. There was an ice cream place next door; sometimes kids waved and smashed their cones against the glass. Salt and Pepper, two tabby boys, entertained them by chasing the drops of melted chocolate and runaway sprinkles that trickled down the pane. The kids called Kat "the mean one" because she ignored them and scolded the other cats for acting foolish and playing along. But when she spotted me, her eyes softened and she would leap from the window and greet me at the door.

Shelter life took its toll on Kat, and after three years, she was diagnosed with kidney failure. She stopped eating, lost a bunch of weight, and almost gave up. Because I was the only one Kat tolerated, the vet asked if I would bring her home for hospice care. I already had a dog and four cats, and taking another one seemed a stretch even for me. But I agreed and at the end of the day, I packed her up and off we went. Sometimes life's timing isn't perfect, but you make it work anyway.

The first night we set Kat up in our spare bedroom. We had a floor-to-ceiling, pyramid-shaped cat tree that we snatched up at a garage sale. The room was tiny, and the cat tree took up most of the floor space. I foolishly thought Kat might like a room and high perch of her own. Other foster cats had, but not Kat. She didn't like being alone or being left.

Kat cried—no, screeched—the whole first night. Our four cats and terrier-mix gathered outside her door, concerned yet curious. At about three in the morning, we broke down and let her out. When the mouthy mystery girl emerged, the others fanned back and let her pass. And then we waited, frozen in place, holding our breath, for the new cat drama to begin.

But nothing happened.

Our apartment was a railroad flat with one room leading into the next. Kat marched down the center like she owned the place, making a beeline for a fish-shaped cat bed in the living room. The other cats paused, then slowly crept back to their safe spots, eyes on Kat, bellies low to the ground. My husband and I went back to bed, and our dog followed. I stared at the ceiling for what seemed like hours, waiting for sounds of feline distress. But there was only stillness.

Kat claimed her favorite spots: the back of the recliner; the cool in the summer, warm in the winter radiator; and pretty much any newspaper we tried to read. Each morning she led the happy cat prance to the kitchen for breakfast, circling my legs like she had been there all along. Guests said she looked younger, like a whole different cat. But she wasn't different, just more herself. Kat was peaceful and clearly felt safe, maybe for the first time ever.

When I was three months pregnant, I took Kat for her quarterly checkup. The vet was cautiously optimistic, reminding me that Kat was living on borrowed time.

We lived six blocks from the vet's office and started walking through morning air that felt like a warm bath. The city streets just waking up, awnings and windows opening, vendors setting up sidewalk tables and displays while commuters rushed to catch buses and cabs. Kat traveled well in her shoulder bag carrier with flaps that opened on all sides like a screened-in porch. She loved to be out and about, breathing in the sun and city smells—last night's spices blended with dark roast, old hardcover books, and pastries.

We passed a garden store with small trees, flowering shrubs, trays of perennials, and statues of fairies and woodsy animals. And that's when I first felt it—a strangeness, not a cramp or hunger rumble, but more of a flutter, almost like a tickle.

Turning on a tree-lined side street, we found a bench and sat down. Kat gazed up through her carrier sunroof with relaxed summer eyes. It was a steamy August day just like the one two years earlier when I first brought her home. But that seemed like forever ago, another lifetime, and I hoped it did for her as well.

I felt it again like a butterfly grazing my arm only inside my core. Kat was with me then and also months later when baby kicks felt more like otters. The vet wasn't sure Kat would live to see the birth of my daughter. But in that moment with the flowering shrubs, pretend Tuscan fountains, and first uncertain flutters, I knew she would, and she did.

Kat surprised everyone by living three years with us. Celebrating holidays; new jobs, neighbors, and furniture; snowstorms and heat waves; morning sickness, labor pains, and colicky nights; and lots of ordinary days that when bound together make years that matter.

We don't always start off where we end up or belong. There are false starts, trial and error, loss and disappointment, broken parts, searching and more searching. Because sometimes home is not some place but someone. A brief moment of sameness, a missing piece we didn't even know was missing.

Kat was our missing piece or maybe we were hers. In the end, it probably doesn't matter. Only that in spite of everything, we eventually all found our way home. Together.

20

C'mon Baby and Rescue Me

Ann M. Green

I never had a cat until I was an adult with children. Parakeets, yes; a dog, once; two raucous little parrots, for way too long. But once I got a cat, I became a cat person. The only kind of cat I've had has been a rescue cat, whether it was Rascal, Miss Peach, Love, or Miss Baby. Each thrums a chord in my heart. My husband was not a pet person, but our sons, Robert and William, and I were, and we wanted one. When we lobbied for a dog, Husband put the kibosh on that idea, so we got a tabby cat instead and told him, "It's our default dog." We named him Rascal.

The boys and I adored Rascal, even to the point of allowing him to drape himself across the top of our parakeets' cage to stare transfixed at them as they stared back like statues. Rascal was the master of our house and our hearts, but he also fell prey to the whims of teenagers.

When Rob and his friend Beth dyed their hair blue and green for Halloween, they nabbed the unsuspecting cat and decorated him too. They were quite proud of their handiwork when they held him up for me to see. I was horrified. Poor Rascal, damp but colorful, licked his paws until his tongue turned green, then he started in on his blue belly. I washed his fur and banned them from the cat. Rascal was nothing if not long-suffering. I rescued *him* this time, but another time, I had to rescue a creature *from* him.

Rascal was an indoor/outdoor cat and enjoyed the birds that showed up on our lakeside patio. We had regular visitations from mallards and Canada geese. If inside the house, Rascal stared from the window and chattered at the ones who wandered near. One spring day when he was outdoors, an errant duckling waddled by. Rascal's instincts told him to dash over and scoop it up in his mouth. Then he stopped stock-still in his tracks with the duckling squawking and flailing in his jaws. Apparently his instincts only went so far because he had no idea what to do next. I imagine him thankful that at least one of us knew. I gently pried open his mouth to rescue the baby, who fled back to the lake to escape its fate.

Another rescue cat from the local shelter we named Miss Peach. She was a sweet kitty with a doleful expression and a matronly demeanor. I'd heard that cats weren't trainable, but Miss Peach learned to do a kitty rollover in anticipation of a treat. Of this I was quite proud. She followed me from room to room just to be with me—or maybe because there was the possibility of a treat. I was spoiled by the attention.

Rob had grown up and moved away but returned for a visit. This time he brought Love, a calico kitty that he named for the feelings he shared with his girlfriend at the time. But Rob and the girlfriend soon parted, Rob left, and Love stayed with me. As large and lumbering as Miss Peach was, Love was small, beautiful, and feisty. They got on well. Like Miss Peach, Love learned a trick; she turned three times in a circle for a treat. The two practiced silent wrestling, which usually started with Love bopping Miss Peach on the head followed by slow-motion wrangling, a frantic finale, and Love walking away. Was she gloating?

Another time when Rob was playing with Love, she scrambled out of his grip, into the outdoors and away. Far away. No sign of her. We spread out through the neighborhood, calling for her. William tacked up signs and went door to door. The irony was not lost on us that we told people we were looking for Love. Since we had no luck finding her, we should have added the lyrics "in all the wrong places." She was gone for good. Spring turned into early summer, and we begrudgingly gave up hope.

Then one warm night through an open window, I heard a stern yeow and opened the front door. There on the doorstep was Love, looking up at me as if to say, "Don't just stand there." She was thin, oily, dirty, and demanding. Where in the world had she been? I nestled her and loved her up good. Then I parked her in the shower, where she had a thorough if very unhappy bath followed by a towel drying, hair dryer, and more snuggling. Confident and assured, she strutted back to reclaim her place in the family.

After Miss Peach passed on, there was only Love. One of my friends had found a tuxedo cat at a local park and brought her home. At first she called the cat Baby, but my friend, being from the South, renamed her more formally as *Miss* Baby. In spite of her sweet name, Miss Baby turned out to be a tyrant. My friend's elderly cat had fled in terror, shivered under a corner hutch, and wet the carpet. The solution was to give Miss Baby to us. On arrival, Miss Baby sniffed the perimeter of our great room studiously with Love right behind sniffing her. Now we had a calico and a tuxedo cat. This could be interesting. Would Miss Baby torment Love? We hoped for a companionable union.

The truth was otherwise. There was not much camaraderie in the form of silent wrestling and tumbling and not much togetherness at all. As insistent as Love was on starting a tussle, Miss Baby was aloof and elegant as an orchid. The closest physical contact they accepted was to sleep on the same bed at the same time, not touching. While Love was content to call our home her world, Miss Baby took every opportunity to dash out an open door. Perhaps she remembered wild times in the park before my friend found her. As soon as she reached the lawn, though, she'd stop abruptly and nibble the grass. It took no time to rescue her—although *she* might not have seen it as a rescue—and bring her back indoors.

Miss Baby was not only aloof with Love, she had been aloof with me too, but I longed to be spoiled with attention. I told myself that some cats just prefer their own company. But after I no longer had Love, the orchid blossomed. Miss Baby inched closer to me. All warm and purring, she jumped up on the couch by me. She climbed on my shoulders and stood on me while I read, which made me laugh out loud.

As it turned out, it was not Miss Baby who was the tyrant; it was the little and mighty Love all along who had orchestrated our lives, wedging herself between Miss Baby and me. With just the two of us, I realized we had the relationship I'd longed for. Miss Baby had become my baby.

21

Endings and New Beginnings

Mary Busha

Noah. That seemed like an unusual name for a cat. But that was the moniker listed on the cage sitting immediately inside the door that blustery February day when we walked into the animal shelter. You couldn't help but glance at the curiously striped cat sprawled out in this obviously placed cage. And glance we did before quickly moving on.

My husband, Bob, and I had come looking to adopt a fluffy black-and-white tuxedo kitten. Checking in at the front desk, we were then ushered down the hallway of windows behind which were a variety of felines. But no tuxedo kittens. Check back, they told us. "New families of kittens come in weekly," one of them said. Deciding we'd return another day, we headed to the door where we would once again pass by the unusually marked cat.

Noah watched as we moved toward the exit. We stopped by the cage momentarily and shot each other looks that seemed to say we really weren't interested. But what would it hurt to have him brought to us in the room set aside to visit potential new family members? If nothing else, we could get a kitty fix until our fluffy tuxedo showed up. And it would give this little guy some playtime outside his cage.

Once we were seated in the visiting room, they brought Noah to us, and he went from Bob to me and back again. Spending a little time with each of us, he purred and rubbed up against us, putting on quite the show. We learned he was a five-month-old marbled tabby. We had never heard of marbled tabbies, but they are distinct, for sure. Once home, I looked up the breed to find out it's not a breed at all. Rather it refers to a cat's color patterns, just as tuxedo refers to cats that are bicolored.

The classic tabby, which Noah was, has bold, swirling patterns along their sides, resembling a marble cake. Many have a pattern of circular smudges on their bodies that resemble a bull's-eye. And Noah surely did.

Within moments, this little guy had won my heart. Even his short hair and unusual markings began to take on beauty in the eye of this beholder. Bob was more amused than taken, but I could tell he at least liked him.

So the cat with the unusual name and markings joined our household, and now there were three of us. When we talked about changing his name, the Bible character Noah came to mind. I pondered what significance that name might have for us; I look for deeper meaning in just about everything. The man Noah for me signified endings and new beginnings. In the story of the flood and the ark, Noah and his family ended their lives in one part of the world when they boarded the ark with two of every kind of living being. They began a new life after a period of time when the ark finally came to rest on dry land.

We, Bob and I, had moved on from our lives in a little town near the thumb of Michigan and had come to rest in Jackson,

Michigan, where we had moved my mom into full-time nursing care. Jackson was a short distance from where my sister lived. She and I could both see to our mom's care.

These were new beginnings for Bob and me. For most of our married life, ministry-related moves had taken us on a journey, zigzagging the country more than a few times. Sometimes we lived in RVs, sometimes in apartments on mission bases, sometimes in the rooms of friends, and in myriad other locations. That came to an end when we returned to Michigan to live near my mom.

With this most recent move, we purchased our own home. And after many years of not being able to have a pet, we now owned Noah. Well, of course, with cats, one always wonders who the owner is.

We started anew with our rescue cat Noah. It was a new life for him too. While we did not know his background, leaving the shelter was a new beginning for him.

That was not an easy period of time in my life. Placing Mom in 24/7 care was one of the hardest things I'd ever had to do. I'd wrestled nearly daily about the shouldas and oughtas in caring for aging parents before and after moving her to a nursing facility. Nearly three years went by before I could leave after our good-bye hugs without feeling guilty. Even though I knew this was the best scenario for Mom, because she loved her new home, it was still difficult. Staff told us that Mom was an example of someone adjusting almost immediately to her new surroundings.

Not only did she adjust quickly, she also enjoyed serving other residents. If they were playing bingo and someone was cold, she would make sure they were covered with their lap blankets or she'd go to someone's room and get their sweater. When it was okay to do so, she pushed others down the hall in their wheelchairs. One day a visitor there to see his elderly parent asked Mom if she was an employee.

So, no doubt, this was good for Mom. I was the one who didn't adjust so well. *You should take your elderly parents into your home, shouldn't you?* Mom's care requirements were more than my sister and I could handle. Bob patiently helped me understand that while we were not personally providing Mom's care, we were seeing that she had good care. Even so, it was hard.

So the solace Noah gave me when I'd return home from my visits with Mom was priceless. When I walked through the door after those visits or from any outing, I'd holler, "Where's my Noah?" From wherever he was, he'd come. Sometimes he'd sprawl at my feet as if to show off that beautiful coat of his. When I sat down, he'd jump up on my lap and purr. If I lay down to nap, he'd curl up at my feet, or rather *on* my feet. Oh yes, this cat brought me comfort every day that he was part of our family.

So while we rescued Noah from the shelter, the moment he entered our home, he was the rescuer. Whether it was coming to me when I called or entertaining us with his kitty antics, he brought us great joy.

In addition, he was good company. In the mornings during my quiet times, I'd sit in my recliner and he'd sit across from me on the windowsill. Sometimes he just stared at me. Mostly he watched the outdoors. I always knew when he saw something of interest by the chirping sound he made when he got excited or spotted a bird.

In the evenings, while we read or watched TV in our favorite living room chairs, Noah most always went to the side of Bob's chair and reached up to him as though asking permission to jump up on his lap, which he always got, of course.

What truly bonded Bob to Noah was their occasional chipmunk capers when the cute little vermin made their way into our home and raced through one of our several rooms. When Noah spotted one, he'd chase and then corner it. Once the chipmunk was cornered, Bob with his trusty piece of cardboard and mesh wastebasket would capture the little critter and then take it across the road where he let it go into the acres of cornfield. Generally, the chipmunks left with half a tail after having been chased, while Noah curled up in a favorite spot and proudly groomed himself. Often I posted about these capers on Facebook with the words: Team Bob and Noah, 1; Chipmunks, 0. I believe one season we got up to Team Bob and Noah, 6; Chipmunks, 0.

And then it was time for another ending and new beginning. After much prayer and consideration, Bob and I decided after five years in Michigan that we would move to Florida to be near our son and his six young children. It was not an easy decision, just as it wasn't easy to move Mom into full-time nursing care. Staff reassured me that if we moved, Mom would be in good hands and that I'd only be a two-hour flight away. In addition, I would be leaving Mom with family close by.

Since we would be traveling and then living in an RV for an undetermined amount of time, we concluded it was time for Noah to have a new beginning too. Bob said it first. "We can't take Noah, you know." His words were no surprise to me. Whenever a major decision is in the works for Bob and me, God always confirms it

---

Classical Cat

The great singer Marian Anderson adopted one of her barn kittens and brought him indoors as a pet. He grew into a sleek black cat whom she named Snoopycat. She made a musical recording, telling his story and singing about the adventures they had together. You can find it online and listen to it: *Snoopycat: The Adventures of Marian Anderson's Cat Snoopy.*

---

in both of us. I had already felt we couldn't take him but didn't have the heart to voice the words.

But what would become of our Noah? Could we find him another good home? We had no intentions of returning him to the shelter, confident that if God's hand was in any part of our move, it was in every part of our move. So I knew that while we didn't have a ready answer, the Lord would provide for our faithful feline friend. So I prayed.

I asked the Lord to bring people to mind that I could at least let know we were looking for a new home for him. Some of my friends were cat lovers too, so I started with them. They said they'd keep their ears open for someone wanting a cat. One of them said that she might have someone interested and asked when we would be letting him go. Since we had just put our house on the market and had no idea when we'd be moving, I told her I didn't know. I couldn't just give up Noah right away. What if it took months to sell? What if our house didn't sell at all? But then what if it sold quickly and we didn't have a new place for him? It was a dilemma I had not considered.

Maybe whoever bought our house would want Noah. But what would be the chances of that? Not everyone loves cats, especially older cats. Even though I knew it was a long shot, I petitioned the Lord that way anyway. When I told our realtor about how I was praying, he looked at me with eyes that were less than hopeful. But he said he'd keep my request in mind when showing the house. And he'd alert the other realtors as well.

Since we put our house on the market in the early part of the year, snow still covering the ground, Bob wanted potential buyers to see pics of our home in other seasons, so he put together a binder with year-round photos. *And* he included a page with Noah's photo, his attributes, and a note that said he too was looking for new owners.

Our house was on the market for eight months. We had several lookers, but no ready offers. I was so glad I hadn't agreed to part with Noah early on. And then one day our realtor phoned to say he had an offer. "And," he said, "they want Noah!" *Yes, Lord!*

He told me that the couple had cats of their own and were adept at integrating felines. What a relief. What an answer to prayer! We would be moving to be near our grandchildren (and did I mention we were exchanging Michigan winters for all-year-long Florida summers?) *and* my Noah would remain in his home with new owners who loved cats. What could be better than that?

I hated to leave my pet of five years. But I knew God had provided the best scenario for him to be able to stay in his own surroundings and for us to be able to travel unencumbered.

A couple of years later, the Lord provided us with another rescue, this time in the form of a seven-year-old miniature poodle rescued from a puppy mill. Our little Missy is quite the girl, but that's for another time and another story.

22

Old Momma and the McGangsters

Vicki Crumpton

Old Momma's story begins in a small wooded area near a busy road in Lone Oak, Kentucky, but it doesn't end there. This is the story of how she became a McGangster and the story of the humans who helped her.

Jim Gatlin and Kevin Headrick are the public faces of a small group committed to improving the lives of feral cats in McCracken County, Kentucky. Both men have always had a soft spot for animals, and cats in particular. Kevin jokes that caring for and rescuing cats is like being in the mafia: "There's no getting out." For almost ten years, Jim and Kevin and others have been feeding and caring for feral colonies. They have their own cats at home as well, of course.

I met Kevin when a server at a local restaurant told me about a cat who might have an injured leg. She wondered if someone could trap it. I asked a friend involved in animal rescue about a trap, and she connected me with Kevin. People who know me think I'm a crazy cat lady. But I have nothing on the McGangster team.

Whether it's brutally hot or bone-numbingly cold, every morning, every evening, every day, Jim and Kevin make their feeding rounds. Jim typically takes the morning feeding, and Kevin covers the afternoons. They began in about 2010 with cats near a local McDonald's and started calling the cats "the McGangsters." The name stuck. Hearing about other colonies, they expanded their efforts and now feed at five locations. These cats get more than food, though. They are trapped, spayed or neutered, vaccinated, and if possible, placed in a loving home. If no homes are available, they're released back into their colonies. Over the years, hundreds of cats have been spayed and neutered. In the early years, Jim and Kevin covered many of these expenses themselves. They do it because they love cats. Now, with social media (the McGangsters have a Facebook page, of course), they have more help with funding and food.

They gathered around them a small network of fellow cat lovers who contribute time, money . . . and copious amounts of cat food. Some of the food goes directly to the McGangsters. However, those who care for other colonies and people in need of help all benefit from donations. In 2019, with grant and endowment funds, the local humane association began offering a free spay and neuter program for anyone caring for over three feral cats. As part of that ongoing effort, the McGangster team aided a local correctional facility in trapping and neutering twenty-three cats and kittens. Their goal is zero population growth in the colonies they care for.

In the hot and humid Kentucky summers, the cats get ice-cooled water and chilled wet food in the evenings. In the cold Kentucky winters, the McGangsters have provided insulated shelters (camouflaged, of course) for warmth.

The cats know Jim and Kevin and their voices. I accompanied Kevin on an evening feeding round. "Where's my babies? Kit, kit, kit, kitty," Kevin called. Some cats came running and pranced and danced and rolled and rubbed the curb in expectation. Others were more cautious. They came slowly from the bushes and trees, behind dumpsters, or beside portable buildings, always alert. Until the food came out, and the canned food especially. Then they were all business.

The McGangster cats are healthy and happy and obviously well fed. Jim says there's no substitute for good and regular food.

Jim and Kevin first met Momma around 2011 at the McDonald's colony. She defied years of efforts to trap her so she could be spayed. A wily and wise gray tabby, she outwitted every kind of trap and every kind of subterfuge. And as a result, she kept producing litters of kittens. Over the years, the humans placed her kittens in loving homes. But Momma always eluded her opportunity for a better life, a forever home. Eight years passed. Kentucky winters and litters of kittens took a toll. She was called Old Momma by now, and her humans knew it was time to ramp up their efforts. She'd produced another litter, and those kitties had been trapped and taken in by an experienced foster. Once again, Old Momma kept avoiding capture. Until . . . one day she got too close to Kevin, and he grabbed the scruff of her neck.

Old Momma joined her kitties at their foster home. Word spread online that she would tame nicely and be available to the right home. A couple from Florida who adopted one of Old Momma's kittens from a previous litter made the drive to Paducah to give Old Momma *and* her newest kitties a life of luxury they'd have never known apart from the work of the McGangsters.

Carol Willis says, "Old Momma McGangster is doing awesome, and her babies have taken over the bed as their playground. They are all so content and spoiled."

Feral cats living rough have a hard life. But thanks to the Mc-Gangsters, Old Momma represents hundreds of cats in the community whose lives have been changed for the better. Many kittens move on to adopted homes. The cats still in the colonies are happy, sheltered, and cared for daily where they live. They've not known anything but their spot in the wild, and not knowing luxury, they are content.

And as the community learns more about the McGangsters and the McGangster cats, they've stepped up to make a difference in their own areas. With local media stories and through social media, people as far away as Arizona have contacted Jim and Kevin to ask for advice. McGangster cats have found homes as far away as Connecticut and Florida. All of this because of two men who love cats.

Helping feral cats has dramatic highs and lows. From injured and ill cats who only know human care when a sad decision has to be made to happy success stories as the cats find their perfect home, Jim and Kevin and their team see and feel it all. It's rewarding, frustrating, thrilling, and heartbreaking. Sometimes on the same day.

Jim and Kevin both say caring for the cats has changed their lives. They both have demanding day jobs. Jim jokes, "See this gray hair? There's no money under my mattress." Jim says caring for the cats has helped him slow down and be attentive to needs. He believes you can judge a person's character by how he or she treats others, especially people and beings who are not as well off.

Kevin finds his feeding rounds to be a stress reliever. He says animals are not responsible for their situations and that people who have enough should help those in need. That's the McGangster way. Kevin says that even in the worst weather, something isn't right about his life if his cats aren't fed. He knows they're waiting on him, and that keeps him going. It's like knowing you have a family to feed. "I'm a sucker for cats in need," he says.

Old Momma's journey began in a wooded area in Lone Oak, Kentucky, and continues in Florida where she's living her dream retirement in the company of two human friends and five of her kittens. Her story reminds us that sometimes we may have a better life staring us right in the face, but all we know is what we know. We shy away because of fear. Sometimes it may feel like we've been grabbed by the scruff of our neck and forced into a new direction. Old Momma's humans know change can be hard. They helped her overcome her fear, prepare to be loved, and to have that retirement home in Florida that she never knew was possible.

23

The Little Cat That Could

Lee Juslin

Someone's knocking on the back door," my husband called to me from the kitchen. When we looked out, there was a little black cat looking up at us wistfully. Later, we would laugh over a cat knocking on the door. Little did we know this was just one of his talents and the beginning of a wonderful adventure.

He was blind in one eye and had one leg that was unusable. From the beginning, L'il B as we came to call him, standing for Little Black, Little Boy, or, sometimes, Little Brat, was different from the other strays we fed just inside our garage. L'il B wanted to explore throughout the garage and hang out with us when we were outside. We put down an old jacket and some towels toward the back of the garage, and he claimed the space as his bed. He stayed in every night, not bothered by the closed door. We even added a couple of catnip mice, which he happily played with.

149

Since the night he knocked on our back door, we suspected he wanted to be part of the family. Then one morning as he stood beside me supervising the filling of the feed bowl, I reached down without thinking and patted him. He drew back slightly, a look of shock on his little face, and I don't know which of us was more surprised. With two terriers and two Scottish Folds, and my husband unemployed, we couldn't bring him inside. Yet, we wanted to do our best for him. Our vet offered to neuter him for a reduced rate, plus a rabies shot, and we stretched our budget for that knowing it would protect him and keep him close. Once neutered, L'il B was no longer attacked by the bigger toms and enjoyed hanging out on our property. He grew to love attention and stroking, and he quickly learned his name.

By summer my husband was employed. Since our household was sadly down to one terrier, we decided to try to bring in L'il B. Neither of us had ever adopted a feral cat, but with guidance from an experienced friend, we got a trap and, one morning, set it up in the garage. L'il B needed first to be tested for feline AIDS and feline leukemia in order to mix with our two indoor cats. Happily he tested negative.

We borrowed a Tokyo cage, something that works well for housing multiple cats, until we could make sure everyone would get along. In only a few days, it was apparent the Scottie and the two Folds were not bothered, and we let L'il B out. He did not run and hide under a bed. Instead, he began to explore the house with all of us trooping behind. He went into a bedroom and hopped up on a windowsill. He checked the bathrooms and the other bedrooms. Then, he came into the living room and settled on the couch. Somehow he knew he was in his forever home.

Sometimes at first, B fell off chairs, off the porch windowsills, off anywhere he climbed because, with only one eye, he lacked depth perception. Those loud thudding falls scared me but didn't bother him a bit. He simply picked himself up and went happily on his way.

Living with a special needs pet was as new for us as living inside was new for B, so we all learned together. The expression on his face the first time he sank his claws into the carpet and couldn't release right away was priceless. His excitement at discovering something new to him but old hat to us made for memorable moments. We learned he loved to play, but certain toys like those with thin cord or line were not good for him. One night we were playing with such a toy, and he managed to wrap the line around his hind leg. He took off like a shot and was finally able to get free, but it made us even more aware that an injury to one of his three usable legs could be very serious for him.

Today L'il B is eight years old and has taught himself to beg like a dog for his dinner. I have taught him to give headbutts on demand. He has also, somewhat reluctantly, assumed the role of head cat over our three younger rescues, often breaking up disputes and giving the youngest a talking to when he gets too rambunctious. B is truly a special guy, and he has revitalized a house with two old fogeys.

Most importantly, L'il B has taught us about handling life's adversities, because he doesn't know he's handicapped or different. The pure joy he expresses at just being alive and among friends is a true inspiration.

24

Not Quite What We Planned

Wendy Lawton

I am a planner. When I decide to do something, I research, look at every angle, and prepare extensively. It's important to me to make the right choice, so when I decided to get my first cat, I went to work. I read everything I could get my hands on about cats. I watched Cats 101 videos to explore each breed of cat and their distinctive traits. By the time I finished, I could tell you which cats are active and need room to climb and run, which cats are good with children, which cats require extensive grooming, and more. Much more.

I finally decided on a Ragdoll cat. They are called that because when you hold them, they practically go limp in your arms. You can cradle a Ragdoll like a baby. They are beautiful—long white fur with Siamese-type points and white feet. They are laid-back, lounging languidly on pillows and soft furniture. It sounded like the perfect, restful office cat for me.

The one thing I forgot to research was how to find said cat. My sister, who knew I was looking for a Ragdoll, called to tell me that someone was selling a litter of Ragdoll kittens on Craigslist. Perfect, right? I called the seller, who was a little vague about the kittens. She said her grandma had one left and if I wanted it, she would meet me halfway, in the parking lot of the Fruit Yard. I know now one does not adopt a kitten in a parking lot, but I was a noob in more ways than one.

As my husband Keith and I met this teenager in the parking lot, I felt as if I was doing some kind of clandestine deal. The tiny kitten was certainly not eight weeks old. She was more like five or six weeks old. A minuscule creature with fluffy white fur, she could fit entirely in the palm of my hand. One eye was red-rimmed and swollen shut, the other was the prettiest blue I had ever seen on a cat. The girl said that something had happened to the kitten's eye . . . maybe another cat bit her eye. She said that because of the injury, her grandma reduced the "adoption fee" to only $60.00.

I asked her what the kitten ate. "Oh, anything" was the answer. I know, these should have been red flags, but I had the tiny scrap of a kitten in my hand. If ever a cat needed a rescue, it was this little girl. I wrapped her in a soft blanket, and we headed home with our little Ragdoll.

The first thing I did when I got home was call our vet and make an emergency appointment. We headed straight out to see about her eye. Dr. Quinley took one look at the eye and shook his head. He said it didn't look good at all. As he pressed open the eye to examine it, a jellylike substance shot out and landed on his lab coat. It looked like the eye itself had ruptured. He gently eased the kitten into his lab coat pocket and took her to the back room to examine the eye more closely. When he came back out, he said he was almost sure the eye would have to come out with the eyelid stitched shut but that he didn't want to do it while she was so tiny. He gave us antibiotic eye drops and pain meds and sent us home.

We named her Molly, the perfect name for such a sweet little kitten. As delicate and gentle as she was, she had no lack of bravery. Keith did the medicating four times a day, and she would snuggle into his hand and accept his ministrations without a whimper. We were in love with our Ragdoll baby, even though the thought of a missing eye made us squirm. It didn't fit in with the perfect cat we'd wanted, but it was too late, she was ours. We sheepishly prayed for healing, not sure if it was right to pray for a kitten when so many friends needed healing far more.

When we took her back to the vet for her recheck, Dr. Quinley was amazed at her eye. It was so much better. He kept moving his hand toward her eye almost as if he was going to hit her eye, testing to see if she could see. She blinked each time. He said, "This is not the same cat, is it?" Of course she was. The infection was gone and the eye looked healthy. Molly had two beautiful blue eyes. The vet couldn't account for it and neither could we, except for the prayers we'd prayed together for our little Molly.

She was perfect in every way. Silver lynx-point nose, ears, feet, and tip of tail with the rest of her body snowy white with even whiter feet. And two big beautiful blue eyes. In those early days, I often put a blue satin ribbon around her neck. She was a little doll, indeed.

As she grew, she became much more kitten-like, feisty and playful. We would try to hold her like a baby, but she always twisted around. She hated being held on her back. Ragdolls were supposed to melt in your arms, but Molly must have missed the memo.

She never seemed languid either. She loved to play with wand toys, which we hung in the pantry. Her favorite was a realistic-looking mouse. We could have played with her for hours if we'd had the time. She never tired of playing—we were the ones who quit first. She would even go to the pantry door, stretch her body as far as she could, and say "mouse." It was so unusual, I even videotaped her saying "mouse" to post on Facebook.

She loved playing in our fenced garden. We made sure to take her out for an hour each day so she could climb trees and chase birds. One day, as I sat and watched her play, I noticed shadows of gray on her body, almost like very, very faint stripes. And her tail seemed to be getting darker. Strange. She was about six months old. I went back to all my research to see if this was normal for a Ragdoll, but I couldn't find anything about shadowed striping on the coat.

As each day went by, those stripes became more prominent. And her fur no longer looked long and fluffy. By the time she was a year old, Molly had turned into a short-haired, gray tabby. All that was left of that tiny Ragdoll kitten were her beautiful blue eyes. How does that happen? It was not what I had planned at all.

No wonder she never melted in our arms. In fact, as she grew out of kittenhood, she also grew out of that sweet disposition. She would lean against or rub against our legs occasionally, but she didn't like to be touched. The only people she tolerated were Keith and me, and the only affection she accepted were scratches under the chin and infrequent pets on her cheeks and head. If visitors reached toward her, they were rewarded with a warning growl, and if they persisted, blood would be drawn.

Our vet remembered the sweet white kitten he carried in his pocket and asked again if this angry tabby was the same cat. When it came time to examine her, numerous towels and vet techs were required. Happily, as she has moved into her third year, she's made peace with the vet and even with some of our visitors.

Molly was ours. Not perfect, not what we had planned, but she was our kitty. As time went on, she grew closer and closer to us. If either one of us was sick, Molly would sit or lie by our side until we were well.

She now walks around the house with tail held high, spending each day with one or the other of us, perched on the chair in Keith's office or lying on the shelf in my office. Though she never lolled on a pillow like a Ragdoll, she is present in a much more powerful way. We now pet her shoulders and sometimes down her back. When no one is looking, Molly crawls onto me to knead my neck, making purring sounds. If Keith walks into the room, she stops immediately, as if she does not want anyone to catch her soft side.

We've come to know her soft side as well as her Molly-ness. She's a complicated creature, not the simple Ragdoll we thought we wanted, but we love her even more for it. She's not what I planned, but as God so often does, he gave us so much more than we thought we wanted.

25

It's Time

Brad Madson

I t's time," the nurse said as she looked at my forehead dripping with sweat.

It was February, right after Minnesota had hosted the National Football League's Super Bowl LXII. I had just completed my twenty-fifth year working for the Minnesota Vikings in community outreach. It was the end of a stressful season for me professionally and personally, and I needed a CAT scan to see what was wrong with my abdomen. That morning I woke up in a puddle of sweat with a nauseous feeling in my stomach. I knew it was time to go to the doctor, but I was terrified what the medical results might say.

"It's time," said my good friend Mary a few weeks earlier. "You've got to stop! You're going to kill yourself. You need something to destress or you need to quit your job. In fact, why don't you get a cat?"

Ah, Mary, the cat-loving advocate. The thought of my getting a pet was absolutely ridiculous. I had no time for a cat. As an NFL team's community relations director, I was one of only thirty-two in the League. It was considered a "glamour job," but if you didn't live and breathe the job eighty hours a week, there would always be someone ready to replace you for half your salary.

The day after I saw Mary, I had a particularly grueling day at work, and my constant nausea made it worse. I wanted to sit on my couch and do nothing. Suddenly, the thought of a soft, furry cat sitting on my lap entered my mind. This began my daily thoughts of calling it quits and retiring early. Even though I was only fifty-six, I was financially ready. I had always lived a frugal life, and since I'd worked twenty-five years, I was eligible to take advantage of a full NFL pension and benefits. It all fell into place. But I didn't know if I was ready.

Fast-forward to my visit to the doctor to learn the results of my CAT scan. The nurse came back with my physician, who diagnosed me with diverticulitis. Even though it wasn't great news, I was relieved I didn't have a death sentence. They said I would need to spend the next several nights at the nearby hospital for treatment.

I was lucky because the diagnosis came when my scheduled vacation was about to begin. I told no one I was in the hospital, not any of my family or friends. I used the time to heal with the support of my medical providers, but also cherished the time to just be by myself and think. When I left the hospital four days later, I had made the decision. It was time to leave the job that had been my life since I was in my early thirties.

I told my bosses about my retirement plans the next week and agreed to stay on for a month and a half, giving them ample time to adjust for my departure and help with a smooth transition. After announcing my decision, I felt immediate relief. I could feel the stress lifting from my body.

Mary was one of the first people I told about my retirement. Instead of congratulations, she said, "Now it's definitely time to get a kitty." If you met Mary, you would understand her obsession with cats. She's the public relations manager at our local humane society, and she lives and breathes felines, always trying to find homeless kitties forever homes.

I resisted her attempts to get me to adopt a cat for the first year. I suddenly had loads of time in my newly found freedom and found myself playing tennis and golf and socializing with friends. Retirement was agreeing with me. Except for one bad habit.

During my working years, I used alcohol to deal with the pressures of work and my insomnia. I began to realize I was drinking too much. I didn't like how I felt and I didn't like wasting money on my drink of choice. One day while looking in the mirror, I decided I had to curtail my drinking. It was time to get physically and mentally healthy.

That same day Mary called me with yet another story of a homeless cat. I had heard cat stories many times from my friend, but this time she sounded desperate and sad. This story was about a cat named Minnie Mae.

Minnie Mae was a homeless stray cat, barely bigger than a kitten, who ended up in an overcrowded animal shelter in northern Georgia. Although she was tiny, she was exceptionally cute. Shelter managers knew if they put her on an animal transport to Minnesota, she would probably be adopted at a shelter up there.

When she arrived in Minnesota, Minnie Mae was scared to death. In her kennel she would hiss at caregivers and veterinarians. She clearly wanted to make sure everyone knew not to touch her. After several days, the year-old gray tabby cat started calming down and eventually started accepting loving strokes. It was at that point that shelter staff decided Minnie Mae should temporarily live in Mary's office, where she could chill in a more relaxed environment with comfortable cat furniture and fuzzy blankets.

After a few days there, Minnie Mae came out of her shell and started soliciting attention. Within a day she was adopted by a family. Mary was relieved the shy and fearful cat was in a loving home.

That relief was short-lived. Within a week Minnie Mae was returned because her new adopter developed allergies. The tabby was once again back in Mary's office. Shelter staff decided to put Minnie up for adoption again but decided she would be shown to potential adopters in Mary's office so she wouldn't have to go into a cage.

Mary took care of the kitty and fielded questions from potential adopters. One particularly educated adopter who was interested in the gray kitty had inquired about Minnie's strange stance and also whether or not she had had a feline leukemia blood test.

The blood test was done on Minnie along with a physical exam. A shelter vet determined the cat had a luxating patella, a condition where her kneecap could become dislocated or move out of place. Fortunately, it was the lowest grade so no one was really worried about it. But Mary was sad to learn Minnie Mae tested positive for the feline leukemia virus.

Although Mary had been around hundreds of cats, she didn't know as much about these kinds of kitties. She researched, googled, and read dozens of articles on the ailment. She learned many felines who are "FeLV" can live long, happy lives, though many have shorter lifespans. It can be safer if they live in homes without other cats, as the virus is transferable by certain behaviors.

Hearing all that, it finally hit me—I was the ideal new roommate! I was having a fresh start at life. Drinking was nearly out of my life along with other unhealthy habits. I wanted someone to care about and someone who needed me. I told Mary, "It's time! I can take her. I want to adopt her. I have the perfect home for Minnie Mae."

Although Mary wanted to find a good place for her office kitty, she was shocked. "Are you sure? You know the cat has to choose you, you don't get to choose the cat. She's also a special needs cat. You've never really had a pet before." She was right, but I insisted on meeting the kitty.

Two days later I went to Mary's office to meet this little girl. I was ready for my introduction and even dressed up to make a good impression. Before we entered her office, Mary advised me to sit quietly, speak softly, and pretend Minnie was not there.

We entered the office and sat in some chairs, quietly talking. Minnie was sitting in a little cubbyhole in the cat tree. I didn't look at her. But within three minutes of my arrival, Minnie came out and wanted soft pets from me. I reached down and rubbed her head. That was it. We bonded instantly!

She was the cutest thing. She had eyes like lime green marbles from my days as a kid. She sat at my feet and tucked her paws under her front shoulders like the Sphinx. I could tell we were meant for each other.

During that visit, I did notice Minnie's luxating patella. Her paw stuck out to the side on her back left leg and looked like a kickstand on a bike. It was cute, just slightly bent off to the side. I decided to change her name to Kickstand, which Mary didn't like. After a spirited, fun exchange, I caved in and said Minnie's name would officially be Minnie Mae Kickstand, or Kiki for short.

Two days later I officially adopted Kickstand, and since then my life has not been the same. She has made an incredible difference in my life and provides me endless entertainment. I feel so relaxed watching her bursts of energy as she flies on top of my furniture and her cat tree.

Of course, there are many unexpected behaviors when you acquire a cat, and we're not just talking about Kiki. When I brought this tabby home, I decided I would give her boundaries. Here's how it went:

Week One: I keep bedroom and office doors closed and off-limits

Week Two: Office door now open

Week Three: Bedroom door open but Kiki not allowed on my bed

Week Four: Allowed on my bed

Week Five: Sleeping on my pillow

Week Six: Kiki sleeping on my bed on her own pillow, which is right next to mine

Despite her feline demands, I have made great strides physically and mentally since Minnie Mae Kickstand (Kiki) came into my life. I have healthier habits, my blood pressure is down, and I express gratitude for my life every day. When football season rolls around, it's no longer an ordeal in which I root for our players but have absolutely no control as a pencil pusher. Instead, I enjoy moments with my new best friend—who is cuddly with me, win or lose.

I can't believe how life's challenges have been eased with the adoption of a rescue cat. Yes, it was definitely time for me to get a cat.

164

26

The Amazing Amelia

Marci Kladnik

One spring, a beautiful eight-week-old shiny black kitten came into my care. She was perfect except for her eyes that were both damaged beyond repair by the herpes virus, a common but nasty affliction suffered by many cats born on the streets.

As a foster volunteer, I had advocated for this kitten even with the knowledge that she might have to be put down. Finding a forever home for a one-eyed kitten is always a challenge; finding one for a totally blind one is a daunting prospect. I asked to have her examined and tested for FIV (feline HIV) and FeLV (leukemia) and promised that, if she passed her physical, I would foster her until a home could be found. Our softhearted nonprofit holder-of-the-purse-strings agreed, and the kitten was dropped off at the veterinary hospital. If all went well, I would be picking her up and bringing her home to foster.

The veterinarian called me personally with the results of the dual tests (negative for both!) and said both eyes would need to be removed, which I had expected. I could hear in her voice as she described how healthy and friendly this kitten was that she did not want to put her down. She told me, "Dogs and cats don't rely on vision as their primary sense the way humans do. They use their keen senses of smell and hearing to compensate and generally do just fine."

Relieved she was healthy and friendly, I agreed to foster the kitten through her recovery following the upcoming surgery and went to pick her up. As the Adoption Coordinator of our nonprofit, I was confident that I could find her a forever home even though it might take some time.

The moment I set the carrier down in my kitchen and opened the door, this kitten boldly stepped out and began exploring her new surroundings with barely a hint of hesitation. I was mesmerized, as was my cat, Nemo "Official Greeter of Foster Kittens," who had come in to check out the new kid. He chirped a quiet greeting to the kitten as she approached.

Within two days the kitten had both downstairs and upstairs mapped out in her tiny head. She knew where the all-important litterboxes were and, of course, the food and water bowls. She scampered up and down the tall cat tree and loved the fresh air and sunshine in the large catio. I sequestered her upstairs in her own room at night, so as to avoid any conflicts with my four resident cats, but since she had tested clean, I did allow some interaction. A kitten needs company, after all!

I dubbed her Amelia after that legendary fearless flyer. I had already fallen hopelessly in love with the kitten and knew she would be staying, although I continued to tell people I was just fostering her.

Four days after she came to live with me, I took her in for the three-in-one surgery—bilateral enucleation and spay. She came home sporting the expected stitches, tubes, and rigid plastic collar. She was also still very groggy from the anesthesia and pain meds, but not so much that she couldn't greet me with a purr.

She slept most of the next three days, often on the window seat in my office cuddled next to my Scottie, Maggie, and Barney, another feline greeter-of-kittens. When she came out of her fog, she was very confused. Frustrated about being trapped in the collar, she repeatedly tried to back out of it. She also seemed to have forgotten the layout of the house. I attributed that to the collar hampering whisker and ear senses. The poor baby had to wear that dreadful thing for three weeks.

Once free of the collar, Amelia dashed around the house chasing the dog, Maggie, and trying to sneak up on the big cats. She remembered where the litterbox was, the treat jar, and my lap. Since she had been blind before her eyes were removed, she didn't miss them and was probably much more comfortable now that they were gone.

Every day Amelia amazed me by adding some new trick to her repertoire, proving she was anything but disabled. She'd scamper up the tall cat tree without pausing and swing herself over the side to shimmy back down. When she ran up the stairs to "her" room, she would make an extra little leap at the top, since she couldn't count. The way she leaped always reminded me of a deer.

Only once did she scare me by going through the railings and walking off the balcony to fall to the hard floor below. I had mistakenly thought she'd check her footing before proceeding, and I felt terrible. Luckily she was fine, just a bit stunned, and I installed barriers all along the balcony.

Playing soccer with her favorite noisy crinkle balls through a room full of furniture was no problem at all. Her hearing was so acute that she would stop short of running into things because the toy had bounced off first. She could even track birds flying across the yard if she were in the catio or leap into the air after a toy tossed over her head. If she did run into something, she only did it once.

Then World War Pee broke out in my house! I don't know if it was because the lack of eyes disturbed my cats (she was unable to read their body language) or if Tweety, the only other female, decided one princess was enough, but someone was definitely *not* happy with Amelia's presence. After a large dog bed and my bed and pillows were soaked on more than one occasion, I got the message. Brokenhearted, I began the search to find Amelia a new home.

At the time I was writing a biweekly newspaper column about cats, so it wasn't difficult to talk my cat-loving editor into letting me write an additional special article. It was the perfect place to tell Amelia's story and plead for a forever home for her. The story ran, but my phone didn't ring.

Amelia was sequestered upstairs, and a four-foot Masonite barrier was put up in the hallway to keep her there. By now she was a four-month-old teenager and she would *not* be blocked in. It wasn't long before I caught her scaling the wall, requiring me to raise it another four inches.

Now she was really upset, and I could tell very lonely. Maggie, Barney, and I spent a lot of time with her, and I let her out into the catio for a few hours every day for some fresh air and sunshine, but I could tell she was missing feline companionship. She especially needed another kitten to wrestle and play with.

A few long weeks later, an adopter came forward, and I drove Amelia to what I expected to be her new forever home. En route my cell phone rang. It was a shop owner in my town saying that someone had just dropped off a tiny kitten found under the freeway overpass. I said I'd take it. A neighbor had a key to my house, so when I returned home without Amelia, I found another black kitten waiting for me in the garage.

That evening and all night long, I was consumed with worry and guilt. Less than thrilled with the home I'd taken Amelia to, I now had the overwhelming feeling that she needed rescuing. Even though I'd have to barricade her upstairs again, I went to bring her home. I knew if I were patient, I'd find the right family for her.

Amazingly, an hour before I left to recover Amelia, I received a call from a couple who had read about the kitten in my newspaper column so many weeks before. They were wondering if she was still available, but they explained there was a potential problem. They had two indoor/outdoor FIV-positive cats on the premises and wondered if it would be a safe environment.

I would be passing their home on the way to get Amelia, so I stopped to meet them and see their house. I was thrilled with both the couple and the layout of the home. I told them I thought it would work with some precautions and that I would stop on my way back home with the kitten so they could meet her.

Just as she had done at my house when I set her down that first time, Amelia immediately started exploring their living room. The couple fell in love with her at first sight, so Amelia and I left them to mull things over and work out an adoption plan.

Now with Amelia back upstairs and the smaller black kitten I'd named Freeway in the garage, my fostering took more hours of the day. Both cats needed companionship. Running up and down stairs all day was great cardio exercise, but I could only spread myself so thin.

Luckily, little Freeway was old enough to be neutered and tested. Testing clean, I introduced the two kittens and let them work it out for a few hours each day until the trilling and playing became more than the hissing and growling. It was only three days before little Freeway was attempting to nurse on Amelia, and she seemed to be enjoying it.

With the bond made, much stress was relieved for all involved, and Amelia quit trying to scale the barrier. However, now I had a new dilemma: the pair needed to be adopted together. I wondered how I was going to break this news to the couple . . .

The weeks dragged by with only a couple of phone calls between us. Finally I was told that the house was being cleaned, the carpets shampooed, and the FIV-positive cats set up to be outside and in a separate part of the house. All good news, but now I had to mention Freeway and hope for the best. I needn't have worried, as there was no hesitation at all. All agreed that there is nothing sadder than a single kitten. I was thrilled, to say the least.

Amelia and Freeway are now adults. The FIV-positive cats have passed on, so Amelia is allowed supervised time in the yard. Her favorite place to lie is by the dish of birdseed on the patio, and she bounces around the lawn attempting to catch the butterflies flitting above her. She has never missed the litterbox. Freeway is now king of the property and still bonded with Amelia.

Amelia's family does not see her as blind, because she doesn't see herself that way. Despite the first rule of "don't move the furniture" when a blind animal is in the home, they do rearrange occasionally. It takes but a single pass for Amelia to adjust her mental map to the new layout. I discovered the same thing when I tested the rule while fostering her.

Amelia got the perfect home! I am allowed visiting rights and it's always a thrill to see Amelia, who, I'm happy to say, remembers me.

Blind animals are a wonder to behold and a privilege to share your home with. The next time I am in the market for a new cat, I will be shopping the "unadoptable" area of the local shelters.

27

That Cat

Lauraine Snelling

When our three kids grew from late grades through high school, we lived out in the country between Vancouver and Battleground, Washington. Our street seemed to be a universal dumping ground for unwanted dogs and cats, especially a quarter mile or so away where there was a patch of woods. Some of these animals ended up dead on the road, I'm sure the coyotes took care of others, but some made it to the homes along the road. Ours often being one of them.

One rainy, blowy day, not uncommon during the winter in the Pacific Northwest, the school bus discharged our three off in front of our house. They dropped their books and jackets in their bedrooms and hit the kitchen—starved as usual. Dusk was creeping over the land soon thereafter when our young teen daughter Marie called me out of the kitchen.

"Mom, come see!"

"Now what?"

She was standing with the outside door partially open to the carport that housed our sixteen-foot red boat that pulled water-skiers in the summer and went fishing or boating about any other time. I followed her out to see a half-grown orange striped kitten cowering under the boat. Bedraggled didn't begin to describe it. The plaintive cries strangled my heart. Marie dropped to her knees to try to catch the cat.

"Just leave it alone, maybe it will go somewhere else. You know how your dad feels about having a cat around."

"Mom, we have to feed it at least." She turned to me, nearly crying. "We can't just ignore it."

My heart was crying with hers. I am a lover of all kinds of animals, and especially any in distress. But we'd not had a cat since our Siamese died of a heart attack years earlier.

Wayne did not want another cat. We'd had several rescues or adoptions but no cats, especially not in the house.

"You'll have to ask your father." Who'd just happened to drive in the yard right then.

Wayne stepped out of his pickup, reached back in for his lunch bucket, and came into the carport.

"Look, Dad, look what just wandered in here." Marie pointed at the kitten.

Wayne rolled his eyes. "You know we don't have kittens or cats here. Just ignore it and it'll move on."

"But Dad, it's starving and so wet and cold. We can't let it suffer like that." She gave him the pleading only-daughter look, tears welling over. "Please, at least I can fix it a box with a towel or something to sleep on."

"Marie, you know if you fix it a box . . ."

"Maybe tomorrow we could try to find it a home."

I could read Wayne's mind. *If you fix it a box . . .*

"Please, Dad, just a box."

The boys both knew that their dad could not turn down his daughter if she wanted something—within reason, of course. His wife knew that too. I always enjoyed watching the exchanges.

He rolled his eyes. "All right, fix a box, and tomorrow find it a home." He muttered his way into the kitchen.

Marie found a spare box and cut out part of one side, then brought an old towel from the ragbag.

"I wish I could dry it off. Do you think it will go in the box?"

I shrugged. "All we can do is try."

Wayne rolled his eyes again and gave me one of his looks that said, *Back me up here.* He knew better. When it came to hurting animals, his wife would always take the animal's side. Of course, I draw the line at snakes and alligators.

Marie took the box out to the carport and then stood watching through the windows in the door. "Maybe if I heated some milk and put the saucer in the box, it might go in."

"I agreed to a box. You know that if you feed it—"

"But Dad, we can't let it starve."

"I know, and tomorrow you said you would find it a home, right?"

"Right." She grinned at him, and soon the kitten was lapping at the milk.

Wayne gave me the defeated dad look. "I don't want a cat."

"We have had mice in the cupboard out there."

"There is such a thing as mousetraps."

"You want a cup of coffee?"

"Yes, but I don't want a cat."

"Maybe it will be gone in the morning." Ever the optimist, that's me.

Marie fed the kitten before leaving for school in the morning, adding a bit of hamburger left over from the night before. The kitten let her pet him.

Rain sheeted the window the next afternoon. The kitten was curled up sleeping in the box.

"I asked around school," Marie said, after foraging in the fridge. "But no takers. We could ask around church on Sunday."

This was Friday.

"He's so cute. He let me hold him just now when I took him some more milk."

She spread peanut butter and jelly on a piece of toast. "I was thinking of a name for him."

I shook my head. "You said you'd find him a home."

"I know. He was cleaning his face with his paw after he finished. How come Dad is so against cats?"

I shrugged. I really didn't know either, but that's the way it was. "Ask him."

We did the weekly pilgrimage to the grocery store, and Marie bought a box of cat kibble with her own money that she'd earned babysitting. *Please, darling daughter, don't get too attached.*

She was sitting on the step in the carport, holding and petting the kitten when Wayne came home. "See how pretty he is now that he's all dried. He likes to be held and petted." Marie smiled up at her father. "I know, I am trying to find him a home."

Wayne set his lunch bucket on the counter. "He has to stay outside."

I kept a straight face. An often difficult feat. "You tell her."

A minute later, I heard her shriek, "Thank you, you are the best dad!" She threw her arms around his neck. "I think we should name him Garfield."

"That cat cannot come inside. He is an outdoor cat." Wayne laid out the plan, and Marie smiled and nodded, all the time petting the cat.

A couple of months later, a horrible ice storm shut down Vancouver and the surrounding area. The world turned crystalline, the power lines succumbed, and we had no heat. A fireplace or a woodstove would have been a lifesaver.

"Mom, it's too cold out there for Garfield. Surely we can bring him in just for a couple of days till this weather goes away." School was closed for the day, as was Wayne's construction site.

"Talk to your dad."

Wayne returned from hauling water for both us and our pigs and chickens, and while listening, he kept shaking his head. "If I find a mess in the house . . ."

"He can come in just for the night and sleep in my room. I'll put him out first thing in the morning."

The storm blew over, our frozen world took time to recover from fallen trees and branches, and Garfield grew and grew and grew.

"You have to set that mousetrap," I insisted to Wayne.

"I will, I will."

A few days later, on a Saturday, Wayne was going out to the barn when he returned to the kitchen holding a dead mouse by the tail.

"But you didn't set the trap."

"No, but I found this on the front step. That cat was sitting there, cleaning his face. He's not full grown and he's already a hunter."

He turned when Marie came in the kitchen, followed by the cat. "See what that cat brought?"

She grinned. "I told you he would be a good cat."

"Must be, he brought you a present."

Marie picked the cat up, cuddled him under her chin, and, eyes shining, said, "Listen."

The purr grew louder. That cat knew how to work the system.

The name Garfield never stuck. For the rest of his life, he was Fatcat. The name fit better. And we never had to set mousetraps again.

28

Bear

Katherine Kern

The day my life changed started just like any other during the ten-year-long stretch I'd been fighting anorexia. I'd stayed up most of the night before, not wanting my meager encounter with food to end. At that time, to me, food was love. The time it took me to eat was sacred. A sandwich easily took six or more hours for me to eat. When I finished, I was filled with despairing sadness and loneliness. I'd been in treatment for anorexia twice before that day. Years of my life were devoted to anorexia, but I seemed unable to walk away from it, even when I came near death. The all-consuming nature of anorexia doesn't leave room for relationships.

And then I met Bear Cat. I came home from grocery shopping to find a small, four-pound silver tabby kitten hiding under the deck by my front door. He seemed so tiny—so scared—so overwhelmed by his surroundings. I could understand—most of my life has been lived in fear of one thing or another. That day, it was as if we were terrified of but curious about the other.

We sized each other up. There was some connection, though I couldn't make sense of it and wasn't entirely sure I wanted to. But the cat and I saw something in each other. He seemed just as starved for love as I was. He demanded I stop and pet him, and he simply refused to be turned away.

I named him Bear because he wrapped his paws around my wrist and moved my hand to his belly to be rubbed—just like a bear hug. Here was this tiny, homeless, hungry, and scared kitten and all he wanted from me was ear and belly rubs? He seemed to decide that he loved me and that was that. I trusted my heart for the first time. From that day on, I began to recover from anorexia. Recovery wasn't a straight line—it required treatment three more times. But with Bear's steady love and the peaceful, safe environment of living with him—the exact opposite of my life up to then—I eventually got better. The tiny, once-homeless kitten led me there.

Day in and day out Bear made me smile—usually exactly when I needed it most. His ridiculous antics made me laugh and admire the little guy with the ginormous attitude. Bear was confident, lived with his whole heart. Some of his greatest hits included chewing my textbooks and my homework, putting a fang mark in just about everything I owned, getting his back paw stuck in a jar of peanut butter, sticking his paw in the toaster to get my attention, climbing the clothes in my closet, stealing every little thing that wasn't bolted down and that he could carry (even a teddy bear ten times his size), knocking the contents of my bathroom shelf into the toilet, getting a plastic bag handle caught around his body, enjoying sitting in the pantry, being the bug-master—but always, and I mean *always*, he was at my side or lying against me.

These things were often about getting my attention—even my love. And my admiration grew as I hoped that one day maybe I'd be that bold. The thing is, he was only that bold around me. When anyone else was in my home, he'd mostly hide. But when it was just me and Bear, he acted a bit too big for his britches. He could be a handful, and I admired him for it.

Bear always raised his tail as he walked toward me—or even when he heard my voice. Instead of hiding when he didn't feel well, he found me for reassurance. I haven't been the poster girl for healthy relationships, but the way he interacted with me—checking in and then doing his thing, only to check back a little later—he was the epitome of a securely attached being. Not only that, but I could wrap my arms all the way around him. He wouldn't feel trapped or get scared—he settled in and savored the time with his momma. He even slept with me in bed. While this stressed me out in the beginning, I came to need that closeness and connectedness to sleep well.

Bear changed everything for me. He taught me to accept love (which came in handy in relation to loving myself and letting my now-fiancé love me). With Bear in my life, I could be happy. I could feel safe. I could finally determine who I was and what I wanted in my life without interference or judgment. Other than expecting my love, Bear had no expectations, didn't judge, and didn't hurt or betray me. When I cried, he never complained about my tears wetting his fur. When I had nightmares, he sat on my back until I became grounded in reality. When I felt unsettled in my body, he acted no differently toward me. He loved me no matter if I weighed seventy pounds or a hundred and seventy pounds. Bear increased my self-esteem enough that I decided to give up my eating disorder—and while it took several years in practice, this was the seed that launched my recovery and I never looked back.

My life didn't change in a moment—or even a year. It was an every-day decision to do the hard thing—motivated by Bear to do better for us both and step outside my comfort zone. I healed by persevering when things got difficult, giving it my all, and remembering who I was on the day Bear and I met and what he meant to me over the years. Loving Bear made me a better person—a more loving person, a more understanding person, someone I am proud to be.

Bear taught me that love has the power to truly change everything. And our love did change everything—not only for a tiny homeless kitten but also for the human who opened her heart to him. Life is funny in that we often get exactly what we need when we need it. Our greatest obstacle is always ourselves. We find what we seek, but only if our hearts are open to it.

29

Avery Loves Reilly

Sandra Murphy

When Avery first met Reilly, she wasn't overly impressed. After all, Avery was a Cairn/Yorkie mix, a diva, and insisted on being the center of attention. Yet here was a stray cat, barely out of kittenhood, and he wanted to be friends.

Due to circumstances beyond her control, Avery had found herself at St. Louis Animal Control's high kill-facility (now closed). It was a fluke that I was there on the right day. One look at Avery's smiling face, and I was in love.

At home, potty breaks were on leash until she was familiar with the yard and had a good recall. As we walked from the front of the house to the backyard, a little cat fell in step with us. Mostly white, with large splotches of brown-bunny fur, he wasn't intimidated by a dog three times his size or the strange person walking her. Whenever we came out the door, the small cat would pop up, seemingly out of nowhere, to stroll along with us. Avery started to watch for him too.

One day, Avery had eaten lunch, a new food with lots of gravy, and the evidence remained on her face. My plan was walk first, clean up later.

The cat had other ideas.

He showed up and stepped in front of Avery. Then he sat up like a squirrel, put a paw on each of Avery's cheeks, and proceeded to lick her mouth clean, then and there. She froze and gave me a look that clearly said, "Help! He's touching me!" She didn't move a muscle until the cat was done.

That day, when we came back inside the house, the cat—who would be named Reilly—invited himself in and never left. He never accompanied us on walks again, but he waited by the door for our return. Each separation was a reunion of sniffs and wellness checks. After all, dog and cat had been apart for as much as half an hour.

During her lifetime, Avery rescued over a dozen cats. If we went out and a stray cat was within sight, she'd throw a fit until I got it and brought it into the house. Once inside, it was no longer her problem. She'd done her part. Only Reilly remained her cat. I was designated the caregiver, and Reilly promoted himself to Head Trainer of Kittens.

Avery slept in a crate at night. When a new kitten was adopted, I found it was a good practice to crate the kitty with Avery. By morning, Avery was thoroughly put out at having to tolerate the interruption of her sleep, but the kitten was acclimated to being around dogs. Reilly had to soothe Avery's annoyance and remind the kitten that such overnights were a onetime thing.

The neighbor had a black Chow, and Avery took every opportunity to bark at him, nonstop. Calling her, shaking the treat bag, nothing stopped the noise. One time when I went to pick her up, I noticed her gums were very pale. We made an immediate appointment with the veterinarian, who thought everything was fine until another dog walked down the hall to an exam room. Avery went into full-blown bark mode, and the vet could see the difficulty she had in breathing. An X-ray showed a slightly enlarged heart.

We got a referral to a teaching hospital, and, thankfully, her tests didn't show any heart problems. The vet and his students gave me the diagnosis before bringing Avery to me. She was just a bit . . . plump. A diet with lots of green beans restored her health. We called it Avery's Fake Heart Attack.

These long days when we were away dealing with Avery's issue were hard for Reilly to understand. But it also brought Avery and him even closer. He was beside her every step when we got home, and she loved the attention. After all, her diva genes ruled.

As she got older, Avery could no longer jump up on the bed. Instead, she slept underneath it. I was always afraid that she would be unable to walk and that getting her out from under the bed would be more than just a challenge. But Reilly slept with her. Each morning, he would make an appearance and meow a couple of times. I'd say, "Get Avery up, it's time to go outside and then eat breakfast." Some days it took longer than others but they'd both come out, Avery leaning heavily on Reilly. He'd provide balance until she was stable. It was one of the most touching things I've ever seen.

On days when Avery's appetite slowed, and she showed little interest in food, I'd tell Reilly, "She has to eat. You show her." He'd sniff the food, take a small bite, and then step back so she would eat too. It always worked.

There are people who will tell you cats and dogs can never get along. Cats are aloof, dogs are too rowdy. Dogs chase cats, and cats scratch dogs to let them know who's boss. These people never had the privilege to watch an unlikely friendship between an abandoned dog and a stray kitten left to his own devices. Avery loved Reilly as much as he loved her. He was an empathetic cat, knowing when his dog friend had a bad day or if a kitten got on her last nerve.

Avery and Reilly taught me a lot. A true friendship is when the other party knows your faults and loves you anyway. Watching Avery and Reilly grow old together, helping each other, was a lesson we all need to learn. Just observing, I got more than I was ever able to give them.

30

Enter Loki

Kelly McCardy-Fuller

I am a stay-at-home mom, soon to become an empty-nester. My son went off to college already, and my daughter leaves in the fall. My husband travels for his job, so when our baby leaves, it's just me. We joke that we can't wait to turn her room into a home gym, but to be quite honest, I am having a hard time with this.

I've read all the books, commiserated with all my peers, and even sought the help of a therapist. (I'm a huge advocate of mental health care.) They all say I need to be proactive and find things to occupy my time *before* she leaves. I just can't wrap my head around life without either of my babies at home.

Enter Loki . . .

My husband, Michael, calls me up one day from his local office and says, "You have to come here and get this cat. The guys say it's been out in the yard for two weeks and looks really bad."

"What do you want me to do with it?" I say. "We can't take in any more animals." We already have two rescue cats, a dog, and a bird.

Knowing full well that once I lay eyes on it, the cat will be ours, Michael says, "I'm afraid it's going to get hit by one of the trucks. Can you just come and get it and take it to the vet?"

"This is a bad idea," I say as I load the carrier into my car.

Arriving at his office I see a mangy-looking cat eating off a paper plate. It has a lot of missing fur, but what's left looks a bit like the markings of a colorpoint Siamese. It has baby blue eyes, very crossed, and a strange curl to its lip. It is vigorously scratching its entire emaciated body between bites of food. I'm not sure I actually want to touch it, let alone take it home, but of course, I do. How can I resist? The scraggly thing comes right up to me. He even purrs! *He must know I'm a cat person.*

The vet can't see me until morning, so I put the cat in isolation from our other pets. I can't possibly leave the poor stray alone, so I sit for hours in our half bath, my heart exploding with sympathy for him. At one point he curls up on my legs and falls asleep as something in the back of my head screams warnings of scabies, ringworm, mange, and flea infestations!

The trip to the vet is not good. Stray male Siamese (notice, I have not named him yet) does not have fleas, thank goodness, but

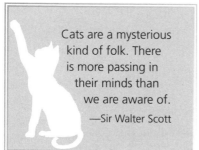

Cats are a mysterious kind of folk. There is more passing in their minds than we are aware of.
—Sir Walter Scott

he has a lot of other problems. He has a skin condition, possibly ringworm, a rotted tooth, thus the snarl, and some sort of severe allergy. He is also estimated to be between eight and eleven years old. The doctor turns around and sanitizes his hands as I cradle the cat up against my chest.

"You haven't had any skin-to-skin contact with him, have you?" he asks. *Oh boy.*

I take a deep breath as the vet jots down some notes. Now comes the hard part that every animal rescuer must face . . . the cost of saving the animal. Skin cultures, sulphur dips for weeks, steroid shots, a tooth extraction including sedation, blood work, and pain meds, and the list goes on. The dollar amount is staggering, and the time commitment is even more daunting.

"I have to talk it over with my husband," I say after the vet tech gives the cat a shot to ease the itch and I buy a bottle of the dip.

"Keep an eye out for any rashes on your arms or chest," she says, and my skin literally crawls.

The next day my arms itch so bad I swear I have ringworm. I'm mortified and call every rescue organization I know. Those that do call me back are either full or can't take an old cat, or a sick cat, blah, blah, blah. I already knew this. We try to do the sulphur dip, which is an exercise in futility, not to mention it stinks to high heaven. It turns the poor cat's fur a putrid yellow color and succeeds in making him look even more pathetic.

The dermatologist says I don't have ringworm and that the arm itching is all in my head. Nevertheless, I am worried about our other pets being exposed. I can't imagine dipping our Siberian Husky in sulphur. Against my husband's wishes, I make the excruciating decision to take the cat to the shelter.

Crying all the way there, I stand in line with mascara running down my cheeks, holding him in the carrier. They give me a ton of paperwork to fill out as every person who walks in glares at me. I swear I hear the word *murderer* whispered by several of them under their breath. After standing in line again, I turn in the paperwork and get ready to hand over the stray.

"Oh, I'm sorry, ma'am, you're at the wrong shelter. You have to take him to the county you reside in." *Oh boy.*

I cry even harder on the way back home, apologizing profusely to the cat as if he knows what almost just happened. I march in the door proclaiming to Michael that I am *not* doing this again. "We are just going to have to get the cat fixed up, whatever it takes," I say between sobs. Michael is visibly relieved that I have returned with an occupied cat carrier, and despite the ordeal, I love my husband even more.

On the morning of his oral surgery, I take Loki to the vet. Loki is named after the trickster in Norse mythology (and Marvel Comics). I ask the doctor to take a look at a strange bump on my cat's ear. He says he will check it out while Loki is under sedation. Several hours later, I'm back to pick up Loki and fork over the money we didn't plan on spending. The vet tells me that the bump on his ear was a BB embedded in his skin. Among all his other problems, my cat had been cruelly shot. Apparently, this is enough to pull at the vet's heartstrings as well, and he cuts my bill in half. Woohoo! Hallelujah!

I spend a lot of time in our half bath the next few months, along with weekly visits to the vet. I find myself tearing up many times while petting Loki and even full-on crying during those hours of isolation in the small room. I recall chanting things like, "It's okay. It's okay. Everything is going to be oooookaaaay. You're my baby. I'll take care of you." I'm pretty sure the waterworks have something to do with the fact that it is already three quarters of the way through my daughter's senior year. Throughout all of the "lasts" we are going through, last football game, last homecoming, last prom, Loki both distracts and comforts me.

When I get the all clear to introduce our new rescue to our other pets, he is a healthy, beautiful cat with one less tooth. Incredibly, Loki is now the most affectionate pet we have. He follows us around and always wants to be on our laps, switching from Michael's to mine and back again at least three times during a nighttime movie. He starts kneading everything in sight, which the vet says is a sign that he is very comfortable here and considers this his home.

Fast-forward to graduation and I'm feeling pretty comfortable too. This empty nest thing isn't going to be as hard as I thought it would be. I have a part-time job, am writing more, and actually feel prepared for my last human baby to leave the nest.

I know the therapist's advice was good, but it is obvious to me now that a certain colorpoint Siamese had a lot more to do with my transformation than she did.

31

SugarBear

Patricia Avery Pursley

Winter had arrived in Texas, and my neighborhood was dark and quiet. Out of my kitchen window, I spotted the brown cat sitting hopefully in a dim circle of light by the garage door. Not having the heart to leave her in the cold, I scooped kibble into a bowl, threw on a down jacket over my PJs, and ventured out to deliver a midnight snack.

When I rattled the kibble and opened the door to the garage, she gave a clipped meow as she sashayed inside, which I interpreted as, *It's about time.* Quickly jumping from the workbench to a shelf, then leaping to a rafter, she peered expectantly at me for room service. I thought it was my night off. Standing on a step stool, I slid the bowl onto the rafter.

Usually the little cat roamed Ann's yard next door. Ann told me that a couple had moved away and left the cat behind. She dubbed it "the brown cat" and added, "I don't need a cat." This cat was neither a thoroughbred nor just a cat. Her Manx lineage was evident by her round shape, bobbed tail, and slightly elevated backside. She was caramel brown with gold and black markings, a thick Manx coat, and what looked like a black question mark on her head. I would soon discover just how unique this little stranger was.

Through the remaining winter nights, I left the garage door cracked open. Most nights she bunked there, and most mornings I was amused to find her prancing on a rafter, expecting breakfast. In the weeks to follow, she spent more and more time in my yard, and I was able to briefly pick her up and pet her. She wasn't shy. If I was working in the yard, she assumed the role of the gardener's apprentice. Every pot was sniffed, every hole dug got a trial run, and every dangling root was given a good swat. She behaved more like a kitten and was as nosy as a dog.

I had already rescued one female cat, Princey, and two rowdy dogs, Burt, a Cockapoo, and Louie, a Westie mix, and it looked like the brown cat was edging in to jump the queue. I considered officially adopting her, but for now, she seemed happy living in the garage. My tree-lined neighborhood of quarter-acre lots was an inviting place for stray cats and dogs. It housed a few chickens, a peacock, and a horse, but was a bit isolating for a busy single woman.

I had a start-up media-relations agency, and I worked long hours from my home office. At the end of a fast-paced day on the phone with authors and the media, my pets helped me wind down. Each one, including the little brown stray, offered a different source of companionship, entertainment, love, and purpose. When I would return from the daily mail run, the dogs would greet me as if I'd been away on a North Pole expedition, and Princey would curl up next to me as I read. As a friend of mine used to say, "You can't beat that with a beating machine!"

One morning when I opened the front door for the newspaper, the brown cat was sitting against the glass storm door. Her wrinkled brow and forlorn look sent the plea, *Can I come in?* Few humans can refuse that feline tactic. I melted. She dashed past me without even a "Hi, how are you?" She ignored the dogs, ran through the living room into the sunroom, and leaped onto the back of a chair to look out the window. It was a friendly takeover, and I was now under new management. Her sunroom acquisition briefly constituted her territory; that is, until she discovered that I slept in another part of the house.

New management or not, she was off to the vet for a checkup and shots. Once on the table, she looked the doctor in the eye, arched her back a little, and did a toe dance. He chuckled and noted that "This cat is round all over!" Indeed, her Manx was showing, and her round hazel eyes signaled "I'm entitled." She bore a strong resemblance to a teddy bear and she had a sweet disposition, so I gave her a one-word name: SugarBear. Syrupy, I know. This cat had distinctive attitudes and moves, including prissy, athletic, and pushy. When she trotted, she flounced along with her tiny behind doing the rumba. She also mastered the clever toddler maneuver, the wet noodle: raise the arms over the head, collapse the shoulders, and slide through Mom's grasp.

She was a daily source of stress-relieving humor for me. At times as I wrote press material, Miss Bear would lounge in my outbox with one paw on the computer mouse; other times she sprawled on the keyboard, presumably waiting for inspiration. Fearless of heights and agile as a Cirque performer, she shimmied right up the giant old oaks in the yard. Near the end of a gnarly branch, she'd lock eyes on me, waiting for my response. The first time she did this I laughed and said, "I see you!" That was her cue, and with ears back, she would whip around and shimmy even higher to challenge me again.

Early one summer, the neighborhood was under siege by a huge, orange bully of a cat, and SugarBear was on his hit list. Catfight yowling caught my attention. I ran outside to discover he had backed her nearly to the end of a branch fifteen feet off the ground. As he crept toward her, she slowly inched backward. The branch started to wobble and bend. I held my breath and knew I had to act fast. I started flinging pebbles at him, which he ignored as they whizzed past. Much to my surprise, one finally caught him on the rump. Divine intervention? He flinched and hightailed a retreat. He never gave up trying to trap her, but she was quicker.

Having survived outside on her own, SugarBear had only one fear, and that was the fierce Texas storms. Usually she would dart under a bed. However, one dark afternoon with thunder and horrific lightning all around, I called Burt and Louie inside. Miss Bear's survival instinct kicked in, and she streaked past me, over the fence, and under another neighbor's shed, a likely hideout from past storms. Rain pelted down in sheets, and golf-ball-sized hail pounded the house. I was concerned for SugarBear out there by herself. A blast of wind brought a sixty-year-old tree crashing across my driveway, blocking the garage door and ripping my sizzling electric lines with it.

After the storm, I learned my neighbor Ann's electricity was still working. We strung a long orange extension cord between the houses. That night, I plugged in a lamp. For the next few nights, parts of the neighborhood were pitch black, including my yard. The car was stuck in the garage, food was spoiling in the fridge, my cat was missing, and I was on my own. My other pets were good company; however, being single meant that I didn't have a husband to comfort me as darkness closed in or to assure me that together we could figure out solutions to the problems at hand.

I walked the neighborhood calling for SugarBear. Silence. I imagined that she may have run off, or worse, was lying injured somewhere. Days later, as the sun was going down, I laughed in relief when I spotted her squeezing out from under Ann's shed and running across the yard. I scooped her up and held her against my cheek. We both purred.

The following year I built a house with clerestory windows that opened high in the family room. Upstairs in an outside wall, I had a tiny cat door installed that exited onto the flat part of the roof. Princey and SugarBear loved slipping out there to sunbathe and survey their kingdom, out of reach of kids and dogs. Quick to adapt, SugarBear saw this as an opportunity to tweak the "I see you" game. Putting on her game face and with nose against the screen, she would peer down, waiting for me to commence saying, "I see you!" Then faster than you could say "cat up a tree," she would gallop to the next window for round two.

Four years and many feline escapades later as my business grew, Dallas experienced ninety continuous days of Texas heat, air-pollution warnings, and Mexican-forest-fire smoke. An executive decision was definitely in order. As long as I had a phone, computer, and fax machine (the good old days), I could live almost anywhere. I decided on Colorado Springs. Ahhh, Pike's Peak, fresh mountain air, cool summers. By then, Burt was no longer with us, and Princey disappeared on moving day. Another story for another day. Soon after I was settled in my Colorado condo, my rumba-dancing cat was quick to create new roles for herself. When I began renovating, she was delighted to assign herself the role of project manager. Rip up carpet? *I can stand on that.* Paint the rooms? *I can sit on spilled paint.* Lay tile? *I can run through wet cement.* Get my drift? The only thing she managed was to get herself in trouble.

Since her outdoor territory had changed again, the adaptable Miss Bear tweaked the "I-see-you" game, this time utilizing the second-story deck railings. Horrified, Mom put an end to that.

Then, one evening, a never-before-seen ancestral streak emerged in said cat. She suddenly dashed out the atrium door onto the deck with much hissing and spitting. The huge raccoon never had a sporting chance. When he spotted this maniac coming, he exited over the side of the deck, where he was hanging on by his nails when I arrived. Who was that cat?

A year and a half later, I met Tom, my husband-to-be. Sugar-Bear doted on him as if *she* were the object of his affection and I didn't exist. When he visited, she sat exclusively on his lap. If she was on my lap at all, it was in passing to get to his lap. One evening as he arrived for dinner, she ran to the door and stood waiting to be noticed. When he finally spoke to her, the raccoon terrorist transformed herself into a smooth-talking siren and began rubbing her face provocatively from side to side against a corner. She tossed him a come-hither glance over her shoulder and did a quick rumba down the hall to the bedroom. She had won him over, and with the help of my little social director, so had I.

After we married, we bought a home in a Denver suburb. Sugar-Bear was about twelve years old by then and politely slept next to our bed on a blanket-wrapped heating pad. Now she busied herself monitoring fox trails in the yard from the night before and peeking through the lattice to see if a new batch of bunnies was in the nursery under the deck. Her high-wire days were behind her.

One Christmas morning, after thoroughly cleaning her face, our sweet kitty with the big personality lay down for the last time on my lap. SugarBear still holds a special place in my heart. I occasionally pull out photos of her lying in the outbox on my desk or posing in oak branches for a game of "I see you!"

32

Flicker

Lonnie Hull DuPont

I t was 9:00 on a summer night when my phone rang. I checked the area code and saw that the call was from a town about a hundred miles away where my good friend Karen lived. But it wasn't her number—it was the number of the medical team that delivered Karen's psychotropic drugs to her apartment twice a day and witnessed her taking them.

Karen was prone to psychotic breaks, and she'd had many hospitalizations for that—some of them recent. Medication would work well for a while, and then it needed adjusting. Lately she had been struggling with hallucinations and hearing voices. This was especially worrisome because she had a history of suicide attempts, though she had not tried to harm herself in many years.

So we continued seeking the right medication and lifestyle for her. And I say "we" because three years prior, my friend had designated me her power of attorney for health issues, including her psychiatric ones. I agreed to it. I knew it was necessary for her to have support, because she lived alone. Not many people were in her life at the time.

She did, however, have a very nice cat. Flicker the Cat had come to Karen when Flicker's previous human, an elderly woman, had to move where she could not have pets. Someone who knew both women intervened when she found out Karen did not have a pet. And Karen agreed to take on Flicker, a senior tabby. Flicker was a big beautiful cat with expressive eyes and the strong tabby markings that made her look as if she were wearing velvety bracelets, necklaces, and belts.

Flicker turned out to be a very good companion, but she had issues. She would hide for days at the slightest provocation. She sometimes groomed so compulsively that she licked her fur right off. She had a seemingly insatiable hunger, panicking when her food bowl was empty. But Karen was very patient with Flicker, and Flicker became devoted to being with Karen.

Now on the phone was a young woman from the medication team. "Have you spoken with Karen today?" she asked.

I kicked myself inside. I spoke to Karen nearly every morning, but today had been unique. From early choir practice before church to dinner with friends to visiting people out of town, this day had been crazy busy and was only now winding down. Karen was usually asleep by now, so I hadn't called her this evening.

"No, I haven't. Why?"

"We went to her apartment to give her evening meds, and she wouldn't let us in. We tried again later, and she still wouldn't let us in. She just cracked open the door and said she wasn't taking meds tonight."

On rare occasions Karen would make the announcement that she wasn't taking meds today, though she always let the medicine people in her home because they were so kind.

"Okay," I said, "I'll call her and call you back."

I hit Karen's number, and she answered in her usual quiet voice. "Hello."

"Hey, there," I said, keeping it light. "Did I wake you up?"

"No." Her voice sounded flat.

"How are you doing?"

"Fine." No change in her voice. Then silence.

"What are you doing?"

"I'm sitting on the balcony."

Red flag. Karen never sat on her fourth-floor balcony. Never. Weather permitting she kept the slider door cracked open to let Flicker sit on the balcony, but Karen herself wouldn't sit out there.

"So why are you on the balcony?"

"I'm waiting for dark."

"Why?"

"I have a rope around my neck. When it gets dark, I'm going to jump." This was said matter-of-factly.

Oh no. I muted the phone and told my husband to call the medication team and tell them to get the police. Darkness was about fifteen minutes away, so I knew I had to be persuasive. I took my phone off mute.

"Karen," I said as calmly as I could muster, "please don't do that. I love you, and I don't want you to die."

Silence.

I tried again. "Would you do me a favor? Would you please take the rope off?"

Silence.

"Please . . . just for me?"

After a pause, she sighed. "Okay, but I have to put the phone down to do it."

I heard her put the phone on the floor, and I prayed hard.

She picked the phone back up. "Okay."

199

"So the rope is on the floor now?"

"Yes." I heard a loud meow. "Something's wrong with Flicker," Karen said.

"Is she on the balcony with you?"

"Yes, and she won't stop crying. She's leaning on my feet and won't stop crying. I don't know what's wrong with her."

I realized we had a secret weapon.

"Maybe she's hungry," I offered. Flicker was always up for eating. "Why don't you go inside and feed her."

"Okay." I was grateful that, although Karen's responses sounded flat, she was open to suggestion. I heard the slider open, footsteps crossing the apartment, and the phone placed on the counter. Then I heard the can of food pop open. After a while, Karen picked up the phone and said, "She won't eat. I guess that's not what's wrong."

"She'll eat eventually," I said. "But listen to me, okay? You need to get your shoes on now because you're going to the hospital. Someone's coming to pick you up. You know you need to go, don't you?"

"Yes, I know," she said. Then I heard a knock on her door.

"That's probably the police to take you to the hospital," I said. "So answer the door and let me talk to them while you put your shoes on."

I heard the booming voice of a policeman, and he took the phone. I told him what was up. I could hear that he was very kind to Karen when he spoke to her. I learned later that he also sneaked onto the balcony to remove the rope and take it away.

The policeman put Karen back on the phone. "Are you okay with this?" I said to her. "You probably need your medications adjusted."

"I know."

I told her I'd make arrangements for Flicker's care, and we hung up. Then I looked at my husband, and I burst into tears.

Karen spent several weeks off and on in the hospital. Eventually new medication made a difference and started to ease her suffering. And one day I could see in her eyes that I had my friend back.

Later on, Karen and I talked about that frightening night. She told me she only remembered two things: my asking her to take the rope off and Flicker's clingy crying on the balcony. "She wouldn't go away from me," Karen recalled. "She leaned on my feet and wouldn't stop crying. She kept distracting me, and I didn't know what to do because I couldn't jump in front of her. I knew if I did, she would be afraid, and I don't ever want her to be afraid."

When Karen returned home, she was on an adjusted balance of medication. She also started seeing a new therapist who seemed to me to be exceptionally wise regarding Karen's issues. I saw improvements in Karen right away. Her voice became more animated on the phone, and she began to socialize once more with her friends and neighbors. She laughed again. She enjoyed leaving her apartment. She worked hard at getting better. As I write this, she has been able to stay out of the hospital.

Another positive thing happened. As Karen improved, we both saw a difference in Flicker. When Karen slept better, so did Flicker. Karen became more social, and so did Flicker—that anxious cat became calmer and began greeting humans at the door, looking them right in the eye.

Karen knew she would still have episodes. She would need to stay on her medication, and she would need to keep talking to her therapist. And she would keep Flicker by her side for as long as possible.

33

Calvin's Gifts

Susan C. Willett

The lights are out. The house is quiet.

On silent pink toes, my cat Calvin sweeps through the house. He is on a mission.

Wearing a cat fur tuxedo any James Bond wannabe would envy, he weaves amid the legs of my dining room table, swiftly navigating toward his objective. He crosses the kitchen floor into the laundry room, where, in a leap of elegance, he lands softly upon the counter.

There, in a basket, lying atop crinkle balls and catnip straws and boingy springs and fuzzy mice are six rectangular furry toys with wide black tails. Two are a deep purply blue with masked faces and felt noses—giving the impression of flat raccoons. Two others are frog-green and sport a wide silly grin. And two more are chocolate-brown with dark eyes and bear ears. These are the

Special Toys. All possess a certain irresistible quality, some unquantifiable essence that draws my cat toward them.

Calvin gently picks one up in his mouth and leaps down to the floor. Unable to contain the anticipatory joy, he starts trotting with a jaunty canter and a proud feline prance back through the kitchen and the dining room. As he travels, he raises his voice in the song of his people, his call barely muffled by the prize he carries in his mouth.

Calvin slows down a bit just as he rounds the corner of the dining room doorway, and then stops as he peers into the foyer. He glances up the stairs; as he moves his head, the tail of his catch sways slightly.

With purposeful and slow strides, he begins to ascend the stairs. Upon reaching the third step, he pauses to deliberate. Here? Or maybe one more? He stretches his neck out and carefully places the blue raccoon toy on the fourth step.

He waits—just a few moments. Considers the placement. Then thinks maybe it's not enough.

The cat turns and runs down the stairs, retracing his steps through the dining room, kitchen, laundry room, leaping again onto the counter, grabbing another toy—a green one—and repeats the delivery, his voice a little stronger along the way, with a touch of plaintive yearning.

This time, Calvin places the frog toy at the bottom of the stairs. Then he sits down. And waits. He hears a stirring from above. The sound of footsteps. He is ready. He is happy. He is a cat who has brought the gifts that will call his human to him.

He starts purring as he hears my door open. He stands up at the sound of my footsteps in the hallway. He calls to me when I appear at the top of the stairs.

"Who's a good kitty, Calvin?" I ask, though I know the answer. "Did you bring me another gift?" I smile as I walk down the stairs, and when I get to the bottom, my cat purrs and meows and rubs my legs.

And so it goes.

Nearly every night, Calvin brings me gifts. Sometimes I hear him and come downstairs to praise my sweet kitty, knowing what an honor it is to be the focus of such devotion. He brings me joy with every raccoon, frog, or bear stuffie he places in the foyer, on the stairs, and in the hallway outside my door. Sometimes he brings one; sometimes there are more stacked neatly in an artful arrangement. Sometimes he adds a selection of additional prizes: a furry mouse, a feathery birdie.

Every once in a while, he leaves his gifts in the dining room or the kitchen; I wonder if perhaps he was interrupted in the middle of a delivery by one of the other cats, who might have hissed him into dropping his offering and scampering to safety under the dining room table.

When I realized his actions had become a nightly ritual, I began taking pictures of each one of Calvin's offerings. I have a collection of more than a hundred such photos.

Every morning, with my first steps outside my bedroom door, I discover what treasures my generous and thoughtful cat has brought me in the night; usually he includes at least one of the flat toys. His is the sweetest, most meaningful gift I've ever had the pleasure to receive. It is a statement of love, a heartfelt effort of devotion.

That's why I come when I hear my cat's recognizable call: to accept his favor in person, to express my appreciation for his effort, and to tell him how much I adore him. To anyone who might ask me who is training whom, who may wish to point out that I'm merely teaching my cat that I'll come when called, I'll say I know exactly what I'm doing.

A few months ago, one of my dogs—an unstoppable, unflappable, ball-chasing terrier named Tucker—was diagnosed with a deadly cancer. We were lucky enough to get Tucker to the vet when he showed some relatively insignificant symptoms (my normally "I'll eat anything" dog wouldn't touch his food), where we discovered internal bleeding caused by the tumors, and rushed him into emergency surgery. After the biopsy results came back, I learned that this particular cancer isn't curable, that the word *remission* isn't even used in relation to it; our veterinary oncologist labeled Tucker's condition as "guarded to poor."

To say I was devastated is an understatement. I have three dogs and four cats, and I love them all, but Tucker is the most alive creature, the most present of my pets. He is part of the posse that follows me from room to room, always by my side. When I enter the house—even if I've only been gone for minutes—his excitement is so overwhelming that he has to grab a toy and hold it in his mouth while his madly wagging back end speaks his joy. He is the most playful and amusing of my menagerie as well, always asking me to throw something for him to chase or rolling around on the floor for the sheer pleasure of it or lying in his dog bed upside down with his paws sticking up and a goofy grin on his face.

We began chemo, which, for the most part, had minimal side effects. But Tucker has some bad days mixed in with his good ones. And so do I. *It's so unfair*, I think. *He's only eight years old.* But then I tell myself that I've been given the incredibly precious gift of time, one that many people don't get with such a diagnosis. I know his life here with me is limited, but I can hug him and hold him and pet him and play with him and feed him his favorite foods and tell him I love him over and over.

But the sadness remains. Some days are worse than others. And it is on those nights—the hopeless ones when I give in to my grief and muffle my tears in my pillow or allow them to fall on the fur of my so-alive terrier—that Calvin brings the most gifts.

Two. Three. Four. An expression of love wrapped in the brightly colored faux fur of his favorite toys.

On those days when he leaves so many, my cat doesn't wait for the acknowledgment. His gift is pure. He doesn't ask for a thank-you or a reward or praise. He is just giving what he can. It is so incredibly touching.

The joys of sharing one's life with a pet are boundless, yet their time on this earth is not. So for now, I'll welcome every moment of faithfulness and trust and love freely given from Tucker, and from Calvin—and from my other cats and dogs. A gift of a raccoon toy upon the stairs is just one of them.

About the Contributors

Kristin M. Avery is an award-winning writer, blogger, and photographer who can be found at www.instagram.com/rubyaroundtown. Kristin serves as secretary for the Dog Writers Association of America and volunteers with several animal rescue organizations. She is currently working on a personal memoir as well as a humorous book about life with pets. She lives in the Chicago area and shares her home with her husband, fourteen-year-old daughter, senior Yorkie-poo, three cats, and two pet mice.

Kristin Billerbeck is a bestselling, award-winning author of over forty novels. Her work has been featured in the *New York Times* and on NBC's *Today*. When not writing, she enjoys good handbags, bad reality television, and annoying her adult children on social media.

Mary Busha is the author of *Breaking the Power of Negative Words: How Positive Words Can Heal* (Revell). Now a full-time writer, speaker, and workshop and event coordinator, Mary spent most of her career working with other writers as editor, publisher, agent, and writer's coach. She is a wife, mother, and grandmother who enjoys reading, crocheting, and leading small groups at her church. She makes her home in Ocala, Florida, with her husband, Bob, and their rescue dog Kaycee, and can be reached through her website: breakingthepowerofnegativewords.com.

Deborah Camp has been a monthly pet columnist for *The Best Times* since 2008—three of her articles earning her sponsored Special Awards from the Cat Writers' Association. She was an editor of the music publication *The Memphis Star*, and for eleven years served as regional executive director for the Grammy Awards organization, NARAS. Her master's degree is in anthropology, and she currently teaches in a graduate program as a part-time adjunct.

Melody Carlson is one of the most prolific novelists of our time. With more than two hundred books and sales topping seven million, Melody writes primarily for women and teens. She's won numerous honors and awards, including the RITA, Gold Medallion, Carol Award, and Romantic Times Lifetime Achievement Award, and can be found at melodycarlson.com.

Tracy Crump is best known for contributing almost two dozen stories to Chicken Soup for the Soul books, and she has also published articles and devotions in magazines such as *Focus on the Family*, *ParentLife*, *Mature Living*, *Upper Room*, and *Woman's World*. She codirects Write Life Workshops, teaches at writers conferences, and edits a popular writers newsletter, and her course on writing for Chicken Soup for the Soul is one of Serious Writer Academy's top sellers. She is also a freelance editor and proofreader for *Farmers' Almanac*, but her most important job is grandma to the world's most adorable grandchildren. Visit Tracy at www.tracycrump.com, www.writelifeworkshops.com (where you can sign up for her newsletter plus story callouts), www.facebook.com/AuthorTracyCrump, or twitter.com/TracyCrumpWrite.

Vicki Crumpton has over thirty years of publishing experience. She holds an MDiv and a PhD and works from her home in Western Kentucky. When she's not taking care of the menagerie, you can often find her riding a bike, paddling a kayak, or taking photos.

Debbie De Louise is a reference librarian at a public library and the author of seven novels including the four books of her Cobble Cove cozy mystery series. Her latest release, *Sea Scope*, is a psychological mystery. She lives on Long Island with her husband, daughter, and three cats. Her website/blog is located at debbiedelouise.com.

Lonnie Hull DuPont is an award-winning poet, editor, and author of several nonfiction books, including *The Haiku Box*. Her poetry can be read in dozens of periodicals and literary journals, and her work has been nominated for a Pushcart Prize. Her nonfiction is frequently about animals, and her most recent book is a memoir, *Kit Kat & Lucy: The Country Cats Who Changed a City Girl's World*. She is a member of Cat Writers' Association and lives in southern Michigan with her husband and two highly evolved cats.

Ann M. Green writes creative nonfiction, video scripts, and plays about local history. She is a retired academic who volunteers for several local nonprofit organizations in the spoken and written word, arts, theater, literacy, and social justice causes.

Robbi Hess has been a lover of pets since she was a child, so she grew up with cats, dogs, gerbils, fish, guinea pigs, and a horse. She has always had a love of words (and of correcting the grammar of others), and both of those passions helped her realize her dream of being a full-time writer. She worked at a newspaper and a business magazine, owned and published her own magazine, and was a frequently published writer of "confession stories." She and her husband share their life with a senior Poodle, a Poodle puppy, a

Goldendoodle, two Devon Rex kitties, a senior rescue cat (Parker), a bearded dragon, and two leopard geckos.

Lee Juslin is a freelance copywriter and the author of the Nurse Frosty series of children's books. She also owns I B Dog Gone, a specialized embroidery business that is dedicated to supporting several terrier rescues as well as her TNR program—the Carolina Cats. Visit her embroidery site: ibdoggone.com and on Facebook www.facebook.com/ibdoggone. Meet L'il B: www.hampshirehooli gans.com.

Katherine Kern is a professional member of the Cat Writers' Association and an award-winning writer/blogger, influencer, and cat enthusiast. You may read about the humorous and touching tales of her two formerly homeless, yet always extraordinary, felines at www.MommaKatandHerBearCat.com; you'll quickly see Kat isn't the "owner" but just along for the ride! Momma Kat and Her Bear Cat also features product reviews and important information for cat parents, and highlights the feline-human bond.

Marci Kladnik, her rescue dog, and three rescue cats live in a small California town with no stoplights or mail delivery. A retired graphic designer and medical technical writer, she turned her talents to championing feral cats in 2007. She sat on the board of directors of Catalyst for Cats from 2007–2013 and wrote an award-winning cat column that ran in three newspapers, which can be read on www.catalystforcats.org. Marci is an award-winning photographer, contributor to www.catster.com, winner of the 2015 Kari Winters Rescue and Rehabilitation Award, and she served as president of the Cat Writers' Association from 2014–2018.

Kristin Kornoelje has had her nose in a book since she learned how to read and has been fortunate to live in the world of words as a book editor for the past twenty years. When she's not reading or editing, she enjoys travel, gardening, live music, and spending time with her friends and family. She lives in Michigan with her two cats, Walter and Millie.

Wendy Lawton is an agent with the much-respected literary agency Books & Such, where she represents some of the finest writers in the industry, including many bestselling authors. As a writer, she won the infamous Bulwer-Lytton competition, authored thirteen books, and ghostwrote several others. But before entering the literary world, she spent thirty years as a world-famous doll designer. Of course, most importantly, she and her husband, Keith, are cat enthusiasts, running after the four feline friends scampering around their California home.

Andi Lehman freelances in diverse markets and writes nonfiction stories, articles, devotions, and grants. An author, editor, and popular speaker, she enjoys working with children and plans to publish a series of nature books for kids. Her education company, Life with Animals, would not exist if Grungy hadn't found his way back to her in Key West, Florida, many years ago. Learn more about Andi and her work with words and animals at Andi Lehman.com.

Leanne Lowe resides in southern Michigan with her husband, Robert, their two children, and three dogs. She is a returning college student in pursuit of a bachelor of digital arts, and she volunteers at the Jackson College Heritage Foundation and Writing Fellows. Their teams created the Michigan Historical Award–winning movie *Going Home*. Her primary occupation and passion are newborn and child portraiture, and her work has been published in magazines and photography books.

Brad Madson resides in Edina, Minnesota, with his feline roommate, Minnie Mae Kickstand, who keeps patrol over her queendom by sunning herself on her panoramic windowsill. Happy in retirement, Madson enjoys getting together with friends and family to share laughs and play tennis, and he often relives past memories with his former teammates from the University of Minnesota tennis team. In addition to writing and leading an active lifestyle, Madson enjoys volunteering at his local cat rescue group, drawing, reading biographies, and telling random strangers jokes that he picks up from *AARP The Magazine*. Brad is a contributor to *Whisker Fabulous*, a cat blog focused on fine feline living.

Maggie Marton writes about dogs, cats, kids, and the environment for print and web publications and on her award-winning blogs, OhMyDogBlog.com and TheZeroWastePet.com. Maggie coauthored the book *Pet Blogging for Love and Money* (January 2020), a guide to launching and running a profitable pet blog. She lives in the Indianapolis area with one dog, two cats, one toddler, and a very patient husband.

Kelly McCardy-Fuller is a freelance writer and the coauthor of the self-help book *Dealing with Depression on Your Own Couch: A Neuropsychologist's Practical Guide*, which she wrote after sixteen years as an editor for a private-practicing neuropsychologist. Kelly is currently looking for a publisher for her first novel, *A Fly on the Wall*, about a fictional FBI agent with psychic abilities. She often travels with her husband, enjoys fitness and gardening, and volunteers her services to the local Meals on Wheels interviewing seniors and writing Senior Spotlights. Kelly resides in Texas with her husband of twenty-one years (Michael), three cats (Fluffy, Hunter, and Loki), one bird (Merlin), and two dogs (Winter and Storm).

Kathleen J. McClatchey is a lifelong lover of most all animals (including humans). She is a university administrator, musician, composer, writer, fiber craftswoman, mother—including of special needs kids—and a wife. She is blessed to live a life filled with interesting beings in beautiful southeastern Michigan, learning and growing, well entertained along the way. She especially enjoys opportunities to creatively express her experiences of the world, and to listen and understand those of others.

Sandra Murphy lives in St. Louis with Ozzie, a Westie-ish dog, and Louie, a black-and-white tuxedo cat, who carry on Avery and Reilly's legend as best friends—eager to play but guarding their food. Fiction stories from Sandy can be found in *Dogs and Dragons, The Eyes of Texas: Private Eyes from the Panhandle to the Piney Woods, The Extraordinary Book of Amateur Sleuths and Private Eye Stories, Mid-Century Murder, The Book of Extraordinary Historical Mystery Stories* (cowritten with Michael Bracken), and *A Murder of Crows*, which she also edited. Read more short stories in Sandy's collection *From Hay to Eternity: Ten Tales of Crime and Deception*. With her real-life pets and imaginary friends, there's never a dull moment.

DJ Perry (www.djperryblog.com) is the CEO of www.cdiproductions.com, an American motion picture company. Several of his screenplays have been produced into award-winning films, including The Quest Trilogy (*Forty Nights, Chasing the Star, The Christ Slayer*), *Wild Faith*, and *Man's Best Friend*, just to name a few. Additionally, several of his screenplays have been novelized into books. DJ's stories in this book and in *The Horse of My Dreams* represent his next steps on his path of writing his own books.

For close to twenty years **Patricia Avery Pursley** was a freelance media relations agent representing Christian authors to national print and electronic media for interviews. Her creativity extended from the Santa Fe Natives sweater brand and designs, to the Cowtown Cookie Company brand, product, and packaging, still on the market today. Currently living in the Houston area, Patricia writes, gets creative in the kitchen, and might be found wandering distant shores with her husband, Tom.

Kathrine Diedre Smith discovered her lifelong passion for animals at a very early age. Growing up in Texas, she and her family had a home in a remote, untamed area where nature and the wilderness nurtured her. She has worked extensively with zoological parks in reproductive physiology and conservation of endangered species, in addition to pursuing her strong passion and skills in animal behavior and strengthening the human-animal bond. Kathrine cares for and manages numerous kitties, feral cat colonies, and wildlife and is deeply committed to animal rescue, as well as inspiring positive changes.

Lauraine Snelling is the award-winning author of over seventy novels, including the beloved Red River of the North series. When not writing she can be found paintbrush in hand, creating flowers and landscapes. She and her husband, Wayne, live in the Tehachapi Mountains in California with their basset Annie and one Buff Orpington hen, Mable, plus two brown Leghorn hens, Maggie and Mary, and a cat named Lapcat who does her best to keep them rodent free.

Claudia Wolfe St. Clair is an artist, writer, art therapist, and *anamcara* from Toledo, Ohio. She is the mother of three and grandmother of six. She and the love of her life are restoring the family home and gardens on Lake Erie. You can read more from Claudia in the Callie Smith Grant collections *The Horse of My Dreams*, *The Horse of My Heart*, and *Second-Chance Dogs*.

Mary Tan is the public relations manager of Animal Humane Society in Golden Valley, Minnesota, the third largest animal shelter in the United States. She also runs a small strategic communications agency called Whisker Media, where she focuses on marketing and public relations for pet-related businesses. When not working, she works tirelessly to change the lives of cats by volunteering at her local cat rescue. The Wisconsin native also writes a blog called *Whisker Fabulous*, which can be found at whiskerfabulous.com and is written from the point of view of her cat, who believes all felines deserve to be fancy.

Susan C. Willett is a writer, humorist, and blogger whose award-winning original stories, poems, and humor appear in print and online, including on her website LifeWithDogsAndCats.com and on Facebook, Twitter, and Instagram. She shares her home with dogs Lilah and Jasper, as well as cats Dawn, Athena, Elsa Clair, and Calvin T. Katz, The Most Interesting Cat in the World™, whose photo went viral and who now has his own social media accounts. Look for Susan's soon-to-be-published novel #*Wheres AzaleaBear* and an as-yet-untitled memoir that captures the joy, wonder, and laughter of life in a multispecies household. Susan has plenty of inspiration for her work, often finding it hiding in a box, splashing through a mud puddle, or taking up an entire couch.

About the Compiler

Callie Smith Grant enjoys animals of all kinds. She is the author of many published animal stories, the author of several biographies for young readers, and the compiler of the anthologies *Second-Chance Dogs* (awarded the Maxwell Medallion by Dog Writers Association of America), *The Horse of My Dreams*, *The Horse of My Heart*, *The Dog Next Door*, *The Cat in the Window*, *The Dog at My Feet*, and *The Cat in My Lap*.

Acknowledgments

I have been privileged to work with a publisher that is not only full of talented people, it's also full of animal lovers. What a pleasure it is to work once again with the team from Revell, a division of Baker Publishing Group. Thank you all.

Special paws up to my patient editor, Dr. Vicki Crumpton. She is the very best.

More paws up for the amazing Cat Writers' Association, an organization full of talent and inspiration.

MORE Stories about the
Cats You Love

Paws to Read Some Stories about
THESE WAGGING FRIENDS

Collections of
Heartwarming Stories
for Horse Lovers

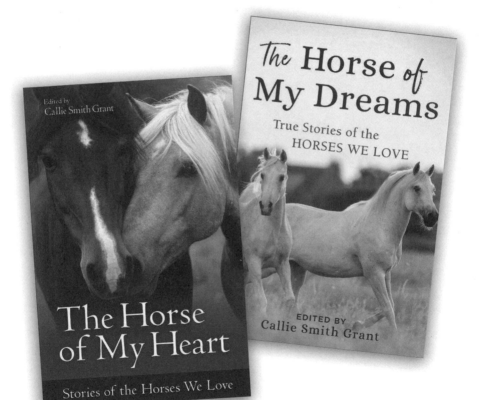

Revell
a division of Baker Publishing Group
www.RevellBooks.com

Available wherever books and ebooks are sold.